PRAISE FOR *HOW TO WRITE EFFECTIVE BUSINESS ENGLISH*
4TH EDITION

'The book helpfully emphasizes that effective writing today isn't just about clarity and conciseness, essential as these are. Today's digital-savvy workforce (and customer base) both expect a great reader experience too. The wide-reaching tips are invaluable, as the author says, "from entry level to CEO"!'
Fabian Schneider, Managing Director, W Ulrich GmbH, Germany

'We today are living in the attention economy, whether it be with your own teammates in companies, your customers, your consumers or even your family. Having the ability to write with clarity, in a compelling way that puts across your point of view and adds value to a piece of communication, is incredibly difficult. To be equipped with the right tools to help people be more succinct and impactful is hugely important in today's world. This book goes a long way in contributing towards that.'
Richard Lawrence, Founder, Innovatr, South Africa

'As a build from Fiona Talbot's previous books, this one deep dives into subjects that are highly relevant when we consider the impact of our written communication today and for the future. I love the references to "power words" that bring our messaging to life, along with the reminder of "staying authentic", "build your own brand" and "show your inner marketer"! There is something for everyone in this book, from early to experienced career, and it's all incredibly relevant within a global organization.'
Julie Brookfield, Head of People, GBG, UK

Fourth Edition

How to Write Effective Business English

Your guide to excellent professional communication

Fiona Talbot

KoganPage

First published in Great Britain and the United States in 2009 by Kogan Page Limited
Fourth edition published in 2023

2nd Floor, 45 Gee Street	8 W 38th Street, Suite 902	4737/23 Ansari Road
London	New York, NY 10018	Daryaganj
EC1V 3RS	USA	New Delhi 110002
United Kingdom		India
www.koganpage.com		

Kogan Page books are printed on paper from sustainable forests.

© Fiona Talbot, 2009, 2016, 2019, 2023

The right of Fiona Talbot to be identified as the authors of this work has been asserted by her in accordance with the Copyright, Designs and Patents Act 1988.

ISBNs
Hardback   978 1 3986 0997 6
Paperback   978 1 3986 0995 2
Ebook   978 1 3986 0996 9

British Library Cataloguing-in-Publication Data
A CIP record for this book is available from the British Library.

Library of Congress Cataloging-in-Publication Data
Names: Talbot, Fiona, author.
Title: How to write effective business English : your guide to excellent professional communication / Fiona Talbot.
Description: Fourth edition. | London ; New York, NY : Kogan Page, 2023. | Includes bibliographical references and index.
Identifiers: LCCN 2023004001 (print) | LCCN 2023004002 (ebook) | ISBN 9781398609976 (hardback) | ISBN 9781398609952 (paperback) | ISBN 9781398609969 (ebook)
Subjects: LCSH: English language–Business English–Study and teaching. | Business communication–Study and teaching. | English language–Textbooks for foreign speakers. | Business writing.
Classification: LCC PE1479.B87 T35 2023 (print) | LCC PE1479.B87 (ebook) | DDC 808.06/665–dc23/eng/20230301
LC record available at https://lccn.loc.gov/2023004001
LC ebook record available at https://lccn.loc.gov/2023004002

Typeset by Integra Software Services, Pondicherry
Print production managed by Jellyfish
Printed and bound by CPI Group (UK) Ltd, Croydon, CR0 4YY

With thanks to my readers and clients, my helpful editor Zexna Opara – and all at Kogan Page, for your interest in the wonderful world of #WordPowerSkills.

Special thanks go to my dear husband, Colin, and to Alexander and Hannah-Maria. A special shout out goes to Johanna and Daren. And to the youngest members of the family, Jude, Dominique, Xanthe and Leander, please continue to take a delight in words. They'll stand you in good stead!

CONTENTS

Introduction 1

01 **Business writing today** 5
We're almost all having to write in business today 5
Who are your readers? 7
What's the purpose of your writing? 8
Readers take just a few seconds to judge your writing 11
How formal or informal do you need to be? 12
Your checklist for action 13
Reference 13

02 **Why are you writing?** 15
Let's get personal 15
Winning business and keeping business: that's why you
write 16
Some principles to help you get started 17
Choosing the right style 23
Ideal communication 27
The Word Power Skills system: four easy steps to premier
business writing 29
Getting a better understanding of 'your inner
marketer'? 30
Your checklist for action 31

03 **It's crucial to connect at every stage of your
career** 33
Effective writing connects people: an even greater must in
hybrid workplaces! 33
Technical writing needs to 'write the talk' 36

Scientific topics can be explained simply to wider
    audiences 39
Pool communication strengths: the rewards of
    generational diversity 41
Write to get that job 42
Write to recruit 43
Use word power to develop your career and get the
    results you need 46
Write for your boss 48
When you're the boss, writing brings extra challenges! 52
Your checklist for action 54
References 55

04   Quality matters 57
What does quality mean to you? 57
Make an honest appraisal! 58
We all make mistakes, don't we? 59
Written mistakes come in many forms 59
Further costs of getting your writing wrong 62
You can never fully outsource your writing 65
Proofreading tips 65
Your checklist for action 66

05   Telling your story through social media 67
Social media has shaken 'the rules' of business writing 67
Get into the social media mindset 67
Get your business message to anyone, anywhere,
    anytime 68
What are the key objectives? 73
How do companies shine through their social media
    interaction? 76
Writing that creates trust can create a community 79
Discoverability with added value 81
Further writing tips for key channels 81
What excites people so much they want to share it? 88

Call people to action – and check it's worked 90
Telling your story 91
Your checklist for action 95

06 Standard or variant English – and changing punctuation and grammar 97
The English language vs business English 97
'Standard' and 'variant' English 98
Writing for both native and non-native English speakers 99
Some surprising problems with English for global business 100
So do define business English within your company 101
Standard or variant punctuation? It's all about context 102
Grammar can change too 108
Paragraphs and other aids to structure 110
Questions 111
Your checklist for action 113
Reference 114

07 Writing globally? Or in multinational teams? 115
Looking at how you use English at work 115
Empathize with the extra challenges for non-native English speakers 120
Collaboration across cultures involves asking if unsure, and sharing tips 121
Some features regularly perplex *all* readers 122
Non-native English writers can have an advantage! 127
Your checklist for action 127

08 Email and instant messaging 129
General 129
Email 131
Writing emails 131

Email scenarios to watch out for 136
Structure your emails 137
Design how you write emails 138
Instant messaging and texting 144
Structure in instant messages and texts 146
Your checklist for action 151

09   Practical conventions and common confusions 155
Dates 155
Time 158
Numbers 160
Measurements 161
Words that can confuse both native English
    and non-native English writers 162
High word count isn't always linked to productivity! 165
Your checklist for action 165

10   Look to the future 167
How does writing make readers feel? 167
Paper is likely to stay around 169
Letters 170
When flexibility is key, be prepared to adapt letter-
    writing 171
A letter that involves the reader with the company's
    narrative 172
CVs/résumés and cover letters 174
Your checklist for action 176
Reference 177

Conclusion: what will you do differently – and better? 179

Index 185

Introduction

English can be the global language of choice in the information and social media age. But how the world of business communication continues to change. In the increasingly dispersed, unstoppable digital workplace, people are discovering more than ever that 'writing is the new talking'. Its tone may be conversational, but its intent has to be to produce the right results. This brings new business performance challenges.

Who is this book for? It's for success from entry-level through to CEO!

Do look to this book if you write in English in any shape or form at work today and want to boost your employability, career development and results.

It'll help you understand how writing is now in effect 'the new talking' – with the new performance challenges this brings, not least in today's hybrid workplace. Written communication leaves a trail by which you are judged, not just at that one point in time when you wrote it. It needs to be tighter than conversation, more business-oriented than chitchat.

This fourth edition of the book has been updated to cover changes in today's fast-moving, ever-changing environment. It is designed for both native and non-native English speakers with intermediate level of written English upwards. (It's not a grammar guide – you'll find plenty of help out there on that.)

You'll benefit from a unique and complete take on the many and exciting manifestations of what effective business English writing needs to look and feel like, across sectors, across generations and across borders.

'One size of English won't fit all' – so I'll show you how to tailor your writing to your target readership, concisely, effectively and professionally.

Companies have under-invested in these key skills and now clamour for them, across the board, across the world.

So what are you waiting for?

It's up to YOU to grab the opportunity here

Invest in your own success, easily and interestingly, via the easy-to-understand four-step writing guidance I show, demonstrated in wide-ranging case studies and everyday work scenarios throughout.

I'm here to help you develop the knowledge and confidence to encapsulate 'your inner marketer' and project your corporate brand. This will enable you to write to:

- influence
- enhance reputation and professionalism
- sell your messages, products and services
- drive effective collaboration
- empathize
- be inclusive
- cut through the noise, and
- improve results

… all in a world of ever shorter attention spans!

Ensure content of value in everything you write

Effective writing today isn't just about reports, presentations, letters and so on. Writing skills arguably matter more than ever in email, instant messaging, the plain English needed for technical documents and coding, marketing, PR, infographics and social media – even in video storytelling and audiobooks where scripts are also key.

Today's need is for content of value and I'm keen that you develop a passion for business writing that creates a consistently good reader experience. And don't let's forget: content means every word you use in every business writing task you do.

Enjoy getting results!

Most importantly, the book is about helping you positively enjoy developing #WordPowerSkills for business success!

Fiona Talbot
Author and consultant, #WordPowerSkills
www.wordpowerskills.com

01
Business writing today

Writing takes centre-stage in the digital age. You need to keep up with the changes.

We're almost all having to write in business today

Picture in your mind someone at work in today's office/home office. What did you see?

Someone writing on the computer, tablet or smartphone? Or someone in a meeting? In that case, there's likely to be some presentation slides and written follow-up, including meeting notes. That's how prevalent business writing is. We just don't always give it that title. It's not just about sales and marketing literature, formal reports and documentation.

How the world has changed over the past years

In a perfect storm of uncertainty, often dispersed teams have to work out new ways to navigate the communication landscape. In the unstoppable digital workplace, people are discovering more than ever that writing is the new talking. But forget chat that goes nowhere. It's about everyone who writes anything at all under-standing that:

- every email, every instant message, every report, every meeting note, every customer-facing correspondence, etc should complete the writing task effectively

- it's about balancing conversation and broadcasting

I'll naturally develop what I mean by this further in the book. But at a glance, do take on board that each individual (so yes, you!) now has to project their talents, market their and their organiza-tion's ideas and build trust in a world of complexity.

It's complex because today's successful organizations arguably put out many more antennae than in the past. Today we largely expect businesses to:

- express where their values lie

- review these on a continuing basis, reacting to internal and external factors

- express in their communication who they support and how active they are in that support

- show their commitment to diversity, gender equality, social justice, climate change and the planet, and so on

Here to help you cope better and enjoy making your mark

It's no wonder people can feel daunted. There's little training out there. The help you find in this book means you and your col-leagues should not only be able to navigate a safe journey through-out all your writing tasks but actually *enjoy* harnessing written word power.

The tried and tested #WordPowerSkills four-step writing system I'll be outlining continues to cover the changing face of communication. The basic principles remain the same, just like these gems of advice from trailblazers of the past:

> If you can't express it simply, you don't understand it well enough. (attributed to Albert Einstein)

> People who think well, write well. Woolly-minded people write woolly memos, woolly letters and woolly speeches. Good writing is not a natural gift. You have to learn to write well. (David Ogilvy, 1982)

Follow the principles I'll outline to:

- relieve anxiety if you're nervous about writing
- support colleagues who find writing hard
- focus on how writing makes people 'feel'
- help you gain the upper hand in your written skills, to get ahead
- prepare you for future jobs and further responsibilities

It's *not* about taking a test or exercises that are right or wrong; it's about getting written words to say what we mean them to say and get the results we need, preferably first and every time.

Who are your readers?

You'll see that I use the terms 'readers', 'target readership', 'customers' and 'audience' interchangeably. A customer can be a person who buys goods or services from a business, or can be a person you deal with in the course of your daily work. The term applies just as much to internal colleagues, suppliers, those in the public sector, etc as it does to those who are external consumers.

Your audience can be anyone and everyone

Where you know your target audience's profile, you have an immediate advantage. Today's business is all about customizing products and services to suit the individual customer. It works for communication too. By what means does your target readership like to receive messages? Are you able to match their needs, generational and cultural expectations, and engage their interest because you know their profile? It's great news if you can.

The potential global reach of your e-writing (which includes social media) is particularly exciting. The start-up business (maybe even operating from home) can have as loud a voice as the large corporate. Your messages may (perhaps unexpectedly) be forwarded on by others, even go viral. So every business message, personalized or not, had better be professional! Nothing should be open to misinterpretation or cause offence, even unintentionally.

Many practical examples and scenarios in this book relate to sales or customer pitches. Because we're all consumers in our private lives, we can relate to and understand these examples. The concepts apply equally to every scenario in the list that follows. Think of lobbying; think of politics; think of charities; think of fundraising; think of promotions; think of the clarity needed for writing clear instructions in coding (one of the fastest-growing career paths in the 21st century); think of the increasing pressure on the medical and legal professions (as just two examples) to write in plain, reader-centred English.

What's the purpose of your writing?

People sometimes think of business writing as a 'soft' skill as opposed to the 'hard' skills of finance, law, IT, etc. But I think this description is misleading. The label 'soft' can give the impression that business writing is an easy skill, and it isn't. Business writing has a critical impact on the whole business cycle; it can win business, it can lose business and it can communicate the framework by which results can be achieved.

So, at the outset of my training workshops, I always take time to ask people why they actually write in their job and what outcomes they seek, individually and as teams. Unless they are marketers by profession, the following aspects of business writing usually come top of the list:

1 to inform or record

2 to cascade information

3 for compliance

4 to seek information

5 to write specifications

6 to achieve a standard

7 to write reports with recommendations

8 to persuade

9 to promote services

Usually far lower on the list (and sometimes only when prompted by me, on the lines of 'Aren't there any other reasons?'), they say:

- to engage interest and involve
- to get the right results
- to sell
- to support customers
- to improve life for customers
- to create a following
- to influence
- to change things/innovate/disrupt
- to enhance brand and reputation
- to show our personality
- to reflect our values
- to eat, breathe and live our vision

Notice how the most inspirational aspects of writing are the ones that are listed as an afterthought!

Why is this? Have bosses become complacent? Are they fostering the false notion that business writing is a boring, lifeless subject? It's so far from the truth! Maybe companies need to focus more on how powerful business writing can be, by asking employees 'What do you write in your social media posts?' The answers are likely to fly back:

'I want to make a difference and be an influencer.'

'I want to disrupt.'

'I want to increase my following.'

'I want likes.'

'I want to make the world a better place.'

'I want to put out the best version of myself.'

'I write about what interests me.'

Now we're getting somewhere. Word Power Skills come naturally in the personal arena. It doesn't have to be so different in a workplace scenario. Encouraging everyone to tap into their 'inner marketer' would soon take the 'boring' out of business writing. When you decide to write things that people will be interested in reading it's likely to enthuse you too.

Activity

Each time you write, first ask yourself:

- Why am I writing?
- What are my/my company's values and objectives?
- Do I have a definite or outline profile for my target audience?
- What are their values and needs?
- How will I align my message(s)?
- What style, vocabulary (and medium, where you have a choice) are likely to suit them best?
- How can I project my company's 'personality' and create an opportunity to show my personality too?

Your writing won't work if you don't first plan what you need to achieve!

Readers take just a few seconds to judge your writing

The written word is unforgiving. When I read, I judge what I see written for what it is. If I'm seeking products or services, what I see can be what I think I get. If it is your writing, I'll judge both you as an individual and your company on the basis of how you expressed yourself at that point in time. And it might not be in your letters or emails or reports. It could be in your presentation slides or the screenshot someone took of your social media post before you realized there was a mistake and hit the edit or delete button. That's how important writing is.

It's commercial folly that many written messages lead to confusion and misunderstanding – even when a company is writing in its native language. Poor writing can also lead to customer complaints. And the worst scenarios are where customers walk away from the companies concerned, and tell others about the bad experience they have received or think they have received. That's the impact that ineffective writing can have. It becomes quite clear that if, as customers, we don't understand or like what supplier A is writing, we prefer to buy from supplier B, who cares enough about our needs to get the message right. And if this takes less time, so much the better.

No body language signals in writing

When we communicate face-to-face, people attach importance to the signals given by our body language. These are said to account for 55 per cent of the impact we make when giving a talk. Our voice can account for perhaps 38 per cent – and our words just 7 per cent (Mehrabian, 1971).

This is because, in face-to-face communication, unlike writing, we don't need to focus just on words. We can ask if we aren't sure what's being said. We can look for clues from the speaker's facial expression or tone as to the gravity or levity of the subject matter. These will help our understanding and focus our attention (or not!).

But in today's workplace written words are *crucial*. Unless the writer is there in front of you, time will elapse before you get answers to any questions you have. That is, if you have the time or inclination to ask questions! At the very least, it means that writers need to think twice, and spellcheck – in fact, double-check – that their words are saying what they mean them to say.

Activity

Are there any writing scenarios and any words that you can think of that:

- have irritated you, or
- have irritated readers generally?

It's worth jotting them down. Discuss with colleagues to gain a consensus. It's a great way to identify effective writing, just a few words at a time!

How formal or informal do you need to be?

As you've just seen, business writing is in a state of flux and is increasingly diverse in style. Generally speaking, the move is towards more 'people' words and more informality.

But this can be a special challenge for some cultures. Asian cultures, for example, place great emphasis on hierarchy, where people of senior grades are treated with noticeably more deference and respect than those in junior grades. Informality can also be a challenge for nationalities where there is a distinction between a familiar and a formal form of the pronoun 'you'. Even Western cultures can do this; for example, French makes a distinction between *tu* (informal) and *vous* (formal). Such cultures can try to compensate for this lack of distinction by writing more elaborately for what they see as the 'formal you' as opposed to the 'informal you'. This doesn't necessarily work.

Luckily it's not rocket science. The answers will be there if you brief yourself on your demographic in each writing task and adapt as necessary. Make sure to look at the words you use and style them towards your target audience.

Your checklist for action

- Recognize writing as an *essential* career skill for you as an individual and for your business.

- Keep up with the changes. Business writing today is much more about 'writing the talk' but we've seen how it's trickier than face-to-face conversation.

- Understand how you can make a difference, even one word at a time.

- Bring your inner marketer to the fore. Improve your writing at every opportunity to impress, influence and boost your employability.

- Remember that English business writing – in its many forms – is your most common route to market. Use the tips in this book to develop your confidence.

- Look at the world around you and see how other people's business writing makes you feel. Consider how you want the people you write to feel. It's a Eureka moment!

- Be the best. You and your readers deserve it.

Reference

Mehrabian, A (1971) *Silent Messages: Implicit communication of emotions and attitudes*, Wadsworth Publishing Company, Belmont, CA

02
Why are you writing?

Get to understand and cover the many layers involved!

Let's get personal

In the last chapter we looked at the many reasons for workplace writing. In this chapter you will be getting a clearer picture of why you write – and just how complex the skill can be.

Take a moment now to list your writing tasks in the box below.

> **Activity**
>
> ....
>
> ....
>
> ....
>
> ....
>
> ....

Is the list larger than you might have thought, especially once you add your daily instant messaging and e-correspondence to your more formal writing tasks?

Winning business and keeping business: that's why you write

Here we have it: there are many layers involved if you really want to deliver the task effectively. We'll shortly look at some typical real-life examples. I'm sure that in each case the writers thought they understood why they were writing. Each one probably thought they succeeded. We'll assess together whether they were always right.

Just before we do this, for those of you who are newcomers to the workplace or are about to enter it following higher education, understanding the difference between academic and business writing will stand you in good stead.

Academic writing compared to business writing

These are two almost entirely different genres. Their goals are different, and they require different approaches.

Academic writing requirements

Students are generally required to write structured essays, research papers and theses. These are largely marked on the basis of how well students have managed to access the right information, process this, show prose/composition skills and accuracy, and conform to a fairly standard presentation format. By and large, the structure involves a beginning (topic and purpose), a middle (evidence and argument, or thesis) and an end (conclusion). The words and tone used must be relevant for the world of academe. This can require a formal, objective, impersonal style and an extensive, specialized vocabulary can gain marks.

Business writing requirements

The workplace is quite different. Yes, you certainly need to know how to access the right information and process this when you write. You need to be accurate too. Many companies still require you to follow a standard house style. But, increasingly, you may be encouraged to make suggestions about how the house style could evolve, in view of business circumstances, customers' needs – and changing communication expectations. This is great news for upcoming generations who can make their mark more quickly than ever before!

Attention spans are lessening, thanks to the 'I-want-it-now' immediacy of the information age. There are fewer occasions for the academic-style beginning, middle and end structure (other than in certain formal reports). Seize the opportunity to develop communication skills that you may not have come across previously.

Some principles to help you get started

What do readers tell us?

Companies who take the time to seek readers' feedback find that readers routinely comment that:

- they feel patronized by poorly written letters
- they can feel insulted by writers' lack of attention to the right detail
- they don't sense the 'human touch' in much of the language used in business writing
- they can feel so angered by correspondence that, where they can do so, they'll walk away from the business concerned
- they dislike unnecessary jargon (words or expressions used by a particular profession or group that may be difficult for others to understand), over-complicated sentences and confusing use of words
- they are offended when their personal details are incorrect

Do re-read this list from time to time. Never lose sight of how readers may react. I'll deal with all these aspects of writing in this book but will just highlight one of the most common now. It's this: what do you think the lack of the 'human touch' in writing could mean? Is it the fact that business writers actively avoid using 'people' words such as 'you' and 'we'? Let me demonstrate. A company writes to a client along the following lines.

Dear Sir,

Re: Policy XYZ

It has come to the company's attention that the aforementioned policy that is about to expire has not yet been renewed. I enclose a renewal form, which you need to return within seven days, otherwise you will no longer be afforded cover.
Yours faithfully,

John Smith

Smith and Co

Some companies still use this stilted, old-fashioned English and I cannot imagine why. Especially now, as we live in a world where customers increasingly expect to feel the personal touch – and to feel valued. So let's redesign the message, using people words and more modern English.

Dear [client's name],

Invitation to renew your policy

We would like to invite you to renew your policy, which expires shortly [date] and would like to ensure that you continue to have the cover you need.

So please could you read, then complete as necessary, the enclosed renewal form, and return it to us by [date]?

> If you have any questions, I'm here to help [telephone number and/or email address].
>
> With thanks,
>
> Yours sincerely,
>
> John Smith
>
> Smith and Co

A letter from my car insurers impressed me easily by ending with a human touch:

> Thank you again for insuring your car with us for another year and we wish you a safe year of driving.

Try to be personable through your writing. People do like it.

So no, don't just write for you and your company

It's true that many companies will ask you to follow a standard house style, with a corporate look and feel to documents. But that doesn't mean you should go on 'auto-pilot' and write robotically.

I'm going to show you why. In the past we saw companies use standard formats for almost every scenario. This can feel wrong today where:

- we expect to innovate and disrupt, to stand out as individuals who want to make our mark and get ahead

- we know our readers expect (even demand) communication that listens to them, is relevant to them and covers their needs

- we expect organizations to keep up to speed on emerging communication trends

Now here's an example showing some of the pitfalls of a standard letter. I've written this as a generic standard letter of the type we often receive as consumers. My imaginary letter is sent by a car insurance broker to a new customer. The context is this: the letter follows on from an initial friendly telephone enquiry in which the customer indicated they wanted to proceed with a car insurance policy at the price quoted to them, and for which they authorized payment then and there. They were told that no documentation was necessary, apart from a signature on the proposal form that the brokers would send by post.

Dear [name]

Re: Private car policy

We enclose the proposal form for your insurance. Check that all the information provided is correct and fill in any missing information. If all is in order, sign the proposal and return to us, for motor insurance policies we require copies of yours and all driver's driving licenses if not already provided. If you have the new style driving licence, send the counterpart section.

Should any aspects of the proposal require explanation, telephone us and we will go through the proposal with you over the phone.

If you have not already made payment by cheque or debit card, return the proposal with your remittance for the premium/deposit as agreed.

Assuring you of our attention at all times.

XYZ Insurance Brokers

If you revisit the context I explained, have you any thoughts as to why this standard letter isn't ideal? What points stand out?

My analysis is along these lines:

1 In this particular case, I suggest this is the unnecessary follow-up:

   a. The customer had previously phoned and spoken to the company, provided all the information requested and paid by debit card. That aspect of the transaction *had been completed* before this letter was sent.

b. In view of this, the letter didn't need to ask for copies of driving licences – yet the customer was inconvenienced by being puzzled by the request and by having to check on this.

c. And there was no need for the letter to refer to any method of payment. The account had already been paid.

2 This standard letter format shouts out to me that this company hasn't kept up to speed with changes in the way we communicate. Where is the 'personalness' that the customer experienced in the previous telephone contact? The headline doesn't even refer to 'Your' Private Car Policy and there's not even a passing reference to the previous telephone conversation.

3 The courteous words 'please' and 'thank you' are missing at every stage of the procedure and there's definitely no thanking the client for their custom. In fact, in what way do they feel valued? As I've just pointed out in the preceding section, we usually prefer to do business with a company that appreciates our custom and *expresses* this throughout the stages of a transaction.

4 They refer to paying by cheque – which is still feasible in many places. But I know of a very recent case at another company, where a customer had their cheque returned with the implication that they were 'a dinosaur': the company no longer accepted cheques. This was despite the company's standard letter categorically stating that it was a valid form of payment. I wonder: are cheques actually still acceptable at this insurance broker? So it makes extra sense that if standard letters are still to be used, they need to be reviewed regularly.

5 If we can see that the wording in this standard letter is robotic writing, it leads to the following question: Is anybody in that office ever going to question the standard format, realizing that it's not actually fit for purpose? It's something for you to think about in your place of work – it may be a way you can make your mark!

6 If the words we write don't mean what we think they mean – or what they ought to mean – we get all sorts of unnecessary and costly follow-up, unwanted by all parties. It could lead to the recipient thinking:

'I'm not sure what I need to do next.'

'Why are they asking for this?'

'This doesn't make sense.'

'This isn't what they told me when I spoke to them.'

'Maybe there's someone better I can go to.'

7 There are grammar points to mention too:

a. They are inconsistent in writing 'licenses' and 'licence'.

b. In this case, 'licenses' is wrong in UK English as 'license' is the verb form and 'licence' the noun (it's worth noting that in US English 'license' is both the noun and the verb form). But this was a notional UK firm – and the second mention of the word 'licence' appears correctly.

c. There should be a full stop/period after 'us', not a comma, in this sentence: 'If all is in order, please sign the proposal and slip and return to us.'

d. A new sentence should start with '*For* motor insurance policies we require copies of yours and all driver's driving licences if not already provided.'

e. But 'driver's' refers to 'licences' in the plural, so grammatically it should be *drivers'* driving licences.

f. They write: 'Assuring you of our attention at all times.' But this is not a sentence and should not have a full stop/period. There is no main verb, so this is a phrase. So standard punctuation would be 'Assuring you of our attention at all times,' followed by a signature.

So can you see that yes, a standard letter, such as this imaginary one, can be useful for the writer as a checklist. It's a prompt as to what needs to be covered in terms of the task. But an effective writer cuts out details that are irrelevant to the reader. Standard

letters can rarely work as a one-off that will sort out all eventuali-
ties. What's more, they can undo the good of previous personable
and customized telephone contact. Never aim for that!

Choosing the right style

More examples follow, showing how writers and readers alike can
be confused by differing styles of written English within their own
company:

1 'Therefore, although obviously we cannot make any assessment
about the matter in hand on this occasion, we will nevertheless
take cognizance of the contents of your letter and will forthwith
forward a copy thereof to the managing director who has the
appropriate responsibility for investigating any issues raised.'

2 'Done.'

3 'Thanks loads.'

The style in the first example is extremely formal English and
quite old-fashioned. You can see what I term *barrier words*:
'therefore', 'obviously', 'nevertheless' and 'forthwith'. They are
all correct English, but they can make readers feel distanced. The
majority of readers will probably view the writer as condescend-
ing towards an 'inferior' reader, rather than communicating with
a valued customer.

  The one word 'Done' in the second example is a common email
response these days, in reply to a question such as 'Have you completed this action?' Those who write the one-word reply usually
feel they are very effective workers and communicators. Once
again what they don't see is the irritated face on the receiving end
of the email! The one-word reply is so often seen as plain rude. Just
by adding four words and changing the reply to 'Yes, I have done
that' can make the writing seem less curt and more polite. As people comment on this in so many training workshops that I run, it's
well worth a mention here.

The third example is very informal and we see it a lot in business today. It's very friendly but be aware some readers may still consider it unprofessional and inappropriate for corporate communication. Some writers say they are only that informal when writing for someone they really know. That's fine. But also be aware there can be a problem when emails may continue in threads – and be forwarded unexpectedly to external recipients too. I've seen time and time again where unguarded colloquial language, including swearing, has caused unintended embarrassment and other problems.

In fact, workplace 'banter' lawsuits are noticeably increasing. It's clearly essential that employers and employees understand that so-called jokey comments about what are termed 'protected characteristics', e.g. sex, age, race, disability, sexual orientation, can amount to bullying, discrimination or harassment and lead to litigation.

Emojis

I'd just like to touch on the use of emojis here. The 'thanks loads' sort of message shown in the last paragraph is often accompanied by 😊.

I wonder what you, and any organization you work for, think about them? It's a fascinating subject, worthy of much discussion in individual places of work. I naturally can't cover this in great detail within the scope of this book.

Emojis were first introduced in Japan. As a country known for its reserved culture, emojis were designed to bring non-verbal clues into written language to help nuance what words meant and to bring personality into communication. Right now, it's considered that emojis are the fastest growing communication tool in history. They don't replace written communication: they are intended to enhance it. But companies need to assess their justified use. Should they be confined to digital textspeak, or can they be used in more formal writing too?

They can be very much welcomed as a diversity tool, as the list is ever-expanding and people can increasingly find an emoji that represents them, culturally and emotionally. That said, you can be entering difficult territory if your reader misconstrues the emoji you have used. Or perhaps you might get it wrong. I have seen someone send the middle finger emoji mistakenly for the crossed fingers emoji. You can imagine the fallout – both sender and receiver were mortified, and a chastened apology had to follow quickly.

You may use them happily in the first instance, not realizing that:

- anybody can misinterpret what you mean or see that you have made an unfortunate mistake

- they can specifically present unfair challenges for neurodiverse people, for example, people on the autism spectrum where it can be an unwanted challenge to interpret expressions

- certain businesses, cultures or customers can be actively discouraged from using them and certain readers/customers can be averse to receiving them

- the list is amplified regularly – digital natives might be able to keep up, but using emojis could actually become a barrier to those who can't, or don't

Have you seen any fallout in the workplace in this respect? Or do you see emojis as a great way forward in projecting your personality and enhancing the tone of your business writing?

Activity

I suggest you discuss this topic in more detail with your colleagues. Also do some research as to how your audience does or does not use emojis.

CASE STUDY   Choosing the right style

Some time ago a major supermarket chain issued a product recall. They had discovered that an axe they sold had a design fault. The head could become detached from the handle.

The retailer decided to ditch the old-fashioned approach to a product recall notice, which in the past might have started:

> A decision has been taken to recall [description of product] as it has been found to be faulty. Please return the product immediately for a refund... [full details of method...].

Instead, they decided to refresh their style and the product recall notice included these words:

> Our [product details] axe would be fantastic apart from the fact that the head can become detached from the handle. Quite clearly, this is not on so we have decided that you need to know. Thankfully no one has been hurt.

They then go on to detail how customers can get a refund. The recall ends with 'It goes without saying... we're very sorry indeed.'

What do you think of this approach? Take a minute to think before reading my analysis.

At first sight, many people quite like it. When they read on, they often change their mind, finding the style too light-hearted for a potentially highly dangerous scenario. And how does the retailer know that nobody has been hurt, just because they hadn't been notified before they posted the recall?

Effective business writing has to 'think ahead' for all sorts of possibilities. It all comes into the 'Why am I writing?' equation – including adopting the right style for the situation as well as the audience.

As a contrast, another supermarket has thought things through in describing one of their cereals in a jokey style: 'DON'T LET BLEARY EYES AND MORNING GRUMPS STOP YOU FROM HAVING A

BREAKFAST BURSTING WITH IDEAS.' It's true that the product could contain allergens dangerous to some, but they are highlighted – and individuals at risk alerted to read the warning. The company does then outline some ideas, as promised.

I wonder if you think such a light-hearted conversational style would work for you or your company?

You are likely to see contrasts in business English writing in the world around you. Consider whether taking a middle course, a median between an overly formal or overly informal style, might work best, to avoid unnecessarily confusing styles.

Ideal communication

It's hard to define ideal business communication but this summary is useful:

> Effective written communication is when the correct, concise, current message is sent out to the primary receiver(s), then onwards without distortion to further receivers to generate the required response.

Let me amplify. Sometimes we write to someone simply to inform them of something. They then remain the primary receiver. The only response we require is that the receiver likes the way we delivered the message (both on a personal and a company level). Probably more often our aim when we write is to do more than simply inform. We're looking for the receiver(s) to like our style and *to do* something too. Our writing should influence them and actively enable this. It's crucial it's understood by all who read it (first-hand or forwarded on) so we achieve our objectives and cover everyone's needs.

Why include the word 'current' in the formula? This is because so often people systematically address the first two points I list, but then forget to update the information. Then the best-laid plans get messed up.

Here's an example. An external trainer is going to deliver a course for 10 members of a company's staff. One week earlier, their manager had issued joining instructions to all attending. The course is to be held in the Byfield Room in a hotel the company uses. The trainer has been emailed the full list of names and has asked the company to notify any changes before the day.

By the day of the training no changes have been communicated and the trainer arrives for set-up. They find that the hotel has changed the venue to the Smithson Room. This hasn't been laid out as requested and there's no overhead projector, which is crucial. By the time the course is due to start at 9 am, only seven attendees have turned up. The trainer texts then calls the company to check but the relevant manager isn't available. So the trainer puts back the start time, in case the missing delegates are held up in traffic.

They later find out that the company knew that three delegates would be unable to attend on the day.

Can you see why the failure to relay changes cost money and affected performance? Both the hotel and the client company were at fault here. Although the course went ahead, there was unnecessary hassle and a distinct lack of professionalism. It also made for a chaotic scene, which was likely to undermine delegates' perception of the whole day. This kind of thing happens all too frequently. It comes as a direct result of people not reading and responding and messaging to update and inform others of changing or changed circumstances. A minor series of events and failure to update communication can turn a well-organized programme into an unprofessional shambles.

Before moving on, I'd like to add another point that I'm increasingly hearing. It's not just ineffective if people don't update written messages, it's seen as rude too. If you can't make it to a meeting, politeness dictates you let the other attendees know in advance and give them the courtesy of your reasons. Effective writing observes etiquette too.

The Word Power Skills system: four easy steps to premier business writing

The system uses the idea of 'a ladder of success', in which you start at the bottom (Step 1) and systematically climb to success (beyond Step 4).

Step 1

Be correct:

- Know what your writing needs to achieve, alongside what your company needs to achieve.
- Reflect your company's values and personality, and project your inner marketer: 'brand you' and stay authentic.
- At the very least, match readers' minimum expectations.
- Ensure that your writing is free of mistakes.

Your business communication will fail if you get your basics wrong.

Step 2

Be clear:

- Use plain English and express facts as simply as possible.
- Edit so that your main points are easily understood.
- Use headings and subheadings to highlight key information.

Confused messages undermine your objectives. They can lose you custom too.

Step 3

Make the right impact:

- Use the right words to grab attention, and a layout that gets noticed for the right reasons.

- Paint a picture with your words and use verbs to convey action and ownership of who does what and when.

- Use the right style to present yourself and your company well.

- Create opportunities.

The right impact differentiates you from competitors and helps bring about the responses you need. There's more about this in Chapter 5 on social media.

Step 4

Focus on readers as your customers:

- Get to know as much about them as you can, so you can write from their perspective.

- Empathize with them and make your content interesting, so that they want to read.

- Favour positive, proactive words to engage, persuade, influence – and create a dialogue and following, where needed.

- Avoid words that put up barriers, and avoid unnecessary jargon.

- Instead, choose words that convey a virtual handshake, to pull people towards you.

Use your written words to satisfy and, if possible, delight your customers.

Getting a better understanding of 'your inner marketer'?

Having a systematic approach like this helps you structure your writing and understand easily the layers involved in writing effectively. The good news is that it can actually be fun projecting 'brand you'. So let me introduce a case study that highlights how to make your writing inclusive and engaging.

CASE STUDY   L'Oréal 'Because you're worth it'

This iconic tagline of global cosmetics company L'Oréal was thought up by Ilon Specht over 50 years ago and still has currency today. It first appeared in two forms: (buy the product) and you validate your self-esteem as an individual 'Because I'm worth it' – and then 'Because you're worth it' is where the company is talking to you.

It was intended to encourage female empowerment, implying that women didn't need to seek approval from anyone but themselves. The campaigns sometimes feature celebrity endorsement but not always, as more recently the tagline has been broadened to the inclusive 'Because we're worth it'.

This is a very neat and very astute tweak of language to extend the reach of the product's appeal both across genders and borders to a massive global audience. It also demonstrates my message that we really can make a difference one word at a time. We're worth that personal development and our readers are definitely worth it. It's a great takeaway message.

Your checklist for action

- Itemize your business writing tasks and objectives; then look at them afresh. The reason that you write in each case needs to be as much from your readers' perspective as your own.

- Realize that your readers and customers are likely to have a negative impression of or even reject *what they see* as ineffective writing.

- Use the four-step writing system shown in this chapter (and which will be demonstrated throughout the book) to structure and foolproof your every writing task.

- Evaluate feedback on your writing. You can do this simply by checking your answers to questions such as the following:
  - o When you send an email or other message, do people often not bother to read it?
  - o Do you have to send out the same message more than once to get the reply you need?
  - o Do people ever congratulate you or complain about the tone of your message?
  - o Are your letters, reports, emails or other messages significantly longer than those of your colleagues (other than for technical reasons)? If so, why is that?
- When you receive new details, do you always update people who need to know?
- Understand the differences between academic writing and business English writing.
- Be prepared to adapt your style but not to the point of confusing your readers. Stay authentic to your personal and company values.

03

It's crucial to connect at every stage of your career

Write accessibly and pool strengths, to connect with readers across disciplines and generations.

Effective writing connects people: an even greater must in hybrid workplaces!

People no longer expect a job for life, faced by economic and post-pandemic uncertainties all around. Employers worldwide are noticing widespread resignations as staff re-evaluate what they want out of life, including their careers. Increasingly people seek something that interests them and expect to reset and develop skills to enable them to move on. What's more, they are making an active decision to avoid 'toxic' workplaces. As I'm showing you in this book, it's no surprise that business writing plays a huge part in making a workplace a nice place to work, or an unpleasant place to work. We can choose words that are effective and hopefully motivate, or we can communicate ineffectively, both adding to our workload and annoying, even demotivating, our readers.

On top of this we see a greater move to hybrid working where employees, now newly working remotely (as international teams have for years), need to develop their soft skills further. They need to learn how to develop relationships with people and even teams they may never meet in person, flipflopping between Zoom calls and the like, instant messaging, emails and more formal documentation.

It's all the more reason to develop great writing skills to boost career prospects. By following the coaching I'm providing in this book, you will be developing the confidence to *be your own coach* – and help others navigate their career success!

Write to connect and strengthen teams

All too often we see disciplines or departments within larger organizations compete with each other in their written communication. You sometimes wouldn't believe they work for the same outfit. Have you come across this?

My advice is simple: appreciate what each brings to the table, pool writing strengths and you'll strengthen teams!

Here's a writing exercise I use in my workshops that brings people together in a surprising way. I ask attendees (from differing professional disciplines) to write a set of instructions for a new entrant to the workplace. It's about telling them how to make a cup of tea, with no vending machine, just the basic ingredients to hand. Out of interest, just jot down in the Activity box how you would approach this.

Activity

....

....

....

....

....

It's fascinating how approaches vary, usually by discipline:

- Those of a technical persuasion tend to start the exercise by describing all the equipment and ingredients needed from the outset, then numbering each step in a logical sequence.
- Some focus on the health and safety aspect: once brewed, let your hot drink cool before tasting.
- Marketers often wax lyrical on making the event an experience: they routinely suggest adding a slice of chocolate cake, then relaxing and seeing how the ideas flow!
- People from other disciplines are often surprised at how layered the approach can be. They are simply not used to being asked to be either technical or creative.

Then at the end, I ask attendees to read out their instructions and we take a vote on the 'best bits' which would then be adopted as best practice, were the instructions ever needed. And guess what? The best bits always include the 'experience' as being as important as the instructions. That to me is the essence of bringing out our 'inner marketer' in our writing.

Analysing differing styles of writing, then choosing the aspects that appeal to all, really brings people together. Do try it and see.

It's no longer time to plough on in a disconnected fashion. It's now a must to join up the dots and findings across all areas of an organization. It's not just about working well in your team; it's about working well with other teams.

Accessibility strengthens connections too

Writing accessibly isn't just about connecting people with words they easily understand. Any writing, whether on websites, in documentation, emails, etc, should be physically accessible to all readers including the disabled. Keep up to speed with what this means. For example, the UK Government issues guidelines on its website to 'Accessible communication formats'. Intended primarily for government communicators, they say it's also useful for communicators in the private and voluntary sector.

Factors to consider include:

- accessible formats with good design and layout
- accessible print to maximize legibility
- a minimum font size of 12 point
- subtitling and signposting to aid navigation through the text

There are other points to consider, such as choosing colours/paper that reduce glare, etc, so do familiarize yourself with what's involved and, as they suggest, research your audience's preferences.

Two examples that regularly get it wrong are very small captions to visuals and restaurant menus in very light grey print that may look stylish but that many find very hard to read. Can you think of anything else?

Technical writing needs to 'write the talk'

But there's no need to let these important considerations bog down your style. For some reason, technical writing can remain resistant to today's conversational style. This is a cue for what comes next!

CASE STUDY   Octopus Energy

Octopus Energy Group is a global energy tech company launched in 2016. The way they write in a technical environment demonstrates many of the principles I recommend in this book. So I suggest you look at their website, in particular their blog entitled *Doing Things Differently* to check out how they have become innovators in this respect.

Some of the main points I'd like to illustrate here are their clear use of headlines not just to help customers navigate the site but also to explain their ethos. Thus we see their claim:

We're doing energy better – for you and for the environment.

By way of explanation, they say they entered the market in 2016 to 'disrupt the status quo with energy that's good for the planet, good for your wallet, and, honestly, good for your soul.'

In this way they are explicitly, but also concisely, stating their values and the widespread benefits they intend these will bring. Then they back this vision with some hard facts when they announce:

… we've been picking up 50,000 customers a month on average, and now supply energy to over 2 million UK homes (and counting). To this day, 92 per cent of our customers rate us as 5* Excellent on TrustPilot… .

In another headline, they set out their store:

Rethinking energy communication.

This is a key component of their ethos. They outline how previously people might have found dealing with energy accounts 'tedious' and 'drudgery'. Their solution? To think about how they communicate as a company, in 'new and exciting ways which can be by encouraging our team to be themselves and talk to customers like they would to their friend or neighbour'.

This means ditching unnecessary formality – which is so often a barrier in customer service. One such example they highlight is to use an unconventional 'Love and Power' message to sign off their emails, not just because it's 'distinctive' to their brand, but also because that's how they want customers 'to feel'.

Elsewhere on their website, they go on to use other differentiating wording, such as swapping the expressions 'credit' and 'debit' on customer accounts to 'above zero' and 'below zero' so that they come over more accessibly to the reader and are less likely to be misinterpreted and confuse.

SOURCE Octopus Energy (nd)

What do you think of this? Does the style surprise you, given the technical subject matter?

My analysis:

1 From the very start, the company focuses on building trust.

2 While modernizing the language they use, they list facts to highlight the credibility they have built up over the years.

3 They explain why they are rejecting formal language.

4 They accept their language is unconventional but commit to it as their distinctive brand.

5 Clear power words are: 'new and exciting ways', 'Love and Power', and 'distinctive'.

6 In a sense 'tedious' and 'drudgery' are also power words. Although negative, they make impact.

An important takeaway is their view: 'It sums up how we want our customers to feel.'

Could you revisit any of your writing in the light of this?

The changing nature of writing for supply chain and other teams

And here's another area of technical writing that's having to adapt. The accepted wisdom used to be that key skills needed at managerial level in supply chain included logical reasoning, financial acumen and great project management skills.

Fast forward to today's world and we see a very clear change. Yes, these qualities are still essential – but we're rapidly seeing the function's importance magnified. It's developed beyond a service function to a *strategic* function too.

So as one example, people who, let's say, were originally appointed for their expertise in delivering accurate and complex spreadsheets, suddenly find this new strategic angle means they too need to be able to write to convince, persuade and sell. In short, it's yet another reason today's business writing needs to draw out 'the inner marketer' in all the ways I'm showing.

Scientific topics can be explained simply to wider audiences

We saw throughout the global pandemic that scientific subjects such as controlling infection and vaccine development had to reach broader audiences than ever before. Here too, audiences expect a more conversational style than in the not-so-distant past. So let's see how successful spoken scientific communication works, so we know how to transpose this into writing.

CASE STUDY   Professor Jonathan Van-Tam

Professor Jonathan Van-Tam was the UK's Deputy Chief Medical Officer up until 2022, and quickly became noted for the freshness of his speeches during government coronavirus briefings.

The BBC commented on how, from pants and football to yoghurts and trains, the Professor had used colourful language to advise people throughout the pandemic (BBC, 2020). This had turned the government adviser into a household name, with many praising how he managed to explain scientific concepts in lay terms.

'I love metaphors. I think they bring complex stories to life for people. It's great,' he told the BBC.

In one analogy, he answered questions from the public, comparing the then current stage of the pandemic to scoring an equalizer in the 70th minute of a football game and went on to say:

It's clear in the first half, the away team gave us an absolute battering, and what we've done now is it's the 70th minute, they got a goal, and in the 70th minute we've now got an equalizer.

> OK, we've got to hold our nerve now, see if we can get another goal and nick it. But the key thing is not to lose it, not to throw it away at this point because we've got a point on the board, and we've got the draw.

He also excelled in expressing calls to action – which are so very important in the business world. At the start of the UK vaccination programme, he urged older people to have the jab, saying:

> I think the mum test is very important here. My mum is 78. She'll be 79 shortly and I've already said to her, 'Mum, make sure when you're called up, you're ready. Be ready to take this up.'

What started as broadcasting soon turned into conversation, as positive reactions quickly came in on writing-driven Twitter, such as:

> Really like listening to Jonathan Van-Tam. He gives a realistic, straight-talking and trustworthy picture, and his analogies are great!

> I'm thinking of starting a little #JVT fan club. He has a way of explaining things that makes sense and he is very authentic in his delivery.

There was a thirst from a worried populace to hear language that resonated with them. The power of these linguistic factors:

- made him come over as *quietly dynamic* (he saw no reason to shout), and set him apart from most every other scientist at the briefings
- made it clear that he is human – to the point he references his care for his mum, and why vaccination matters to him and his family too
- made the messages easily identifiable to the general public
- made the messages not just clear but also easy to *recall*
- made clearly expressed calls to action, giving *compelling reasons* why they were needed

This shift was greatly welcomed. Solid science combined with great public relations yielded such a result. The Professor proved to be a real influencer in this regard. By ditching 'the boring' he injected interest: 'Why does what he's saying matter to *me*, and us all?'

This winning style should absolutely overlap into written communication with wider audiences.

Pool communication strengths: the rewards of generational diversity

Now let's look at how to write across today's multigenerational workplace.

To have up to five generations in today's workplace and client base yields great advantages in different communication perspectives – and successful organizations manage to create a winning fusion of their styles. Interestingly, Millennials and post-Millennials – whom I prefer to call 'upcoming generations' – are estimated to become 75 per cent of the workforce by 2030. They enter the workplace knowing they have a voice. Understandably, they expect it to be heard.

So what advice can I give *all* generations about their writing? Well, until fairly recently, new entrants to the workplace were expected to mirror the writing style of their seniors. Not that long ago young graduates would write to clients, 'We await your instructions at your earliest convenience' and the like. Though it wasn't their natural language, they complied with convention and deferred to their managers.

How times have changed! Broad trends show that upcoming generations are unlikely to be attracted to an organization that doesn't use the accessible language they're familiar with. They also prefer to work for someone they trust, which they'll glean via the values they see communicated.

They noticeably communicate all the time, not so much by phone calls or meetings, but yes, by written words – in instant messaging or emails. Being kept in the loop comes naturally to them and is a key skill that their bosses from previous generations desire, but don't always manage.

In turn, upcoming generations must learn how to write successfully with preceding ones at work, as well as for multigenerational client bases. They must secure buy-in to messages and persuade – especially where the preceding generations may hold greater influence, experience and purchasing power. Where the majority of communication around us today is actually noise, this in itself can lead to a loss of structure. As a result, older managers can complain that younger generations don't always get to the point. The latter can complain that organizations aren't consistently communicating the values they say they're committed to.

Business communication is ineffective and actually unhelpful if it doesn't lead to action, reaction or results. Now more than ever, generations need to work together in the challenging balancing act of getting writing to work. Ditch any generational banter which often overlaps into negativity, such as 'OK, boomer!' (younger to older readers) or 'you whippersnapper you!' (older to younger recipients).

The rewards of sharing perspectives positively via generational diversity are high.

So too are the rewards of analysing how to write at each stage of your career, as I'm now going to show.

Write to get that job

In the first step in your career cycle, research and get a feel for the brand of the organization you're applying to. Then use the #WordPowerSkills writing system shown in Chapter 2 to promote 'brand you'. There's also more help on CVs/résumés later on. But here, let's focus on: What can you best deliver? What will you be passionate about in the job you seek? Why that organization?

In any written interaction with a prospective employer, cover these aspects. Don't then overlook the equally important bits such as:

- matching your answers to all the questions asked
- vetting for mistakes
- caring about presentation

Write to recruit

Attraction

Growing organizations hire. Once in, you may have to help to recruit others to join too. And here things are changing. Employers need to *entice* new recruits and try to avoid costly high staff turnover. Yet again business writing plays a crucial role.

Whether you use an agency or write job ads in-house, everything needs to align with your corporate communication and values.

Also, alongside professional networks such as LinkedIn, tech-savvy, potential new-entrant employees will be looking for work via Twitter, Facebook and other channels. They're likely to be showcasing their talents on Instagram, YouTube, Snapchat and ever-emerging platforms. Check these out to get a feel for what it would be like to work with them. In turn, they will be checking out how (or if) you showcase your business – and making judgements whether *they* are interested in *you*.

Communicate your values – show how you give something back

Stay credible in everything you write. Even if you hire a recruitment company, your organization is ultimately responsible for all wording used. Get it wrong and people notice.

Remember, today's workplace entrants generally expect:

- openness, fairness and social responsibility
- authenticity
- a good and caring workplace experience
- development on the job

Is there anything else you would add to this list? What can your organization offer?

CASE STUDY   Communicating complex ideas simply

Let's look at wording used at Nationwide, the world's largest mutual financial institution. In the past we would have expected traditional writing there. But if we analyse their current language we find an inclusive strapline: 'Everyday people, helping everyday people.' This inclusivity concept is consolidated in articles on their website that contain a strong community slant. Their media advertising follows through, and they even feature real-life clients reciting original, modern short-form poetry to showcase their personality. In this way Nationwide demonstrate a tangible commitment to word power.

They manage to communicate complex ideas in very simple terms. Their mission and values are summed up as PRIDE (itself an acronym that cleverly implies diversity), as follows:

What are our **PRIDE** values?

Putting our members and their money first

Rising to the challenge

Inspiring trust

Doing the right thing in the right way

Excelling at relationships

It's valuable to tune in to how companies are successfully adapting yesterday's language to today's needs. You'll find it a real eye-opener.

Writing must underpin the candidate experience

So many organizations get this so wrong – and the generations who know how to use their voice will quickly share this with others. Posting a great ad is only part of the candidate experience that you will be judged on. Effective writing is courteous and it's expected throughout the recruitment process. It acknowledges applicants' submissions, keeps them in the loop, with all time frames set out and adhered to. And don't forget, upcoming generations won't be expecting (or even wait?) to hear from you in three weeks' time when three hours can seem like ages to them! Ditch the procrastination: speedy emails or instant messaging fit the bill here.

Effective writing also congratulates them if they succeed, and thanks them for their interest even if they don't. Sounds obvious? I'm pleased you think so. Just make sure your organization complies. It really can set you apart for all the right reasons.

Don't be set apart for the wrong reasons as one company recently found to their cost. Managers communicated to colleagues on their internal email that they were going to reject one candidate's application and mistakenly cc'd the candidate into this. This mistake went viral.

This viral event led to others confessing that they too had been copied into hurtful emails. And we see this type of mistake, relaying sensitive information wrongly, happening over and over again.

See what I mean about the importance of how business writing makes your readers feel? And how easily misjudged communication can contribute to toxic workplaces?

Use word power to develop your career and get the results you need

Mid-career and onwards is a time to ensure your business writing doesn't lose its vitality to sell your messages, whatever your business. Keep up the momentum to propel your career forward.

Step 3 in the writing system in Chapter 2 comes into its own right now. Carefully chosen and powerful words don't just sell products or services: they also sell the personalities behind them. In turn they enable the desired responses from colleagues and client base alike.

To give you an idea of powerful words that engage, energize and persuade Figure 3.1 shows a list of words that delegates at my workshops consistently cite, with relish.

What words do you see as valuable power words in your chosen career path? If you're not currently using them, then why aren't you? Start now! Effective writing mid-career can very much be about getting the right mix of blending in and making your mark, to get noticed for the right reasons.

A word of caution: only use power words validly. A finance director in a major retail company who wrote an email to his team exclaiming 'work is fun!' found the reaction much less positive than he expected. Such words may be right for employees in Silicon Valley – but they just didn't feel right for his audience. Another director who emailed 'I'm fired up about this project! Let's work together to get it going' got the team fully involved. Those words, and that inclusivity, worked for them.

Figure 3.1   List of power words

Activity

My at-a-glance power word list

What power words do you like here? What sets you buzzing? What would fire up your readers for the right reasons? What other words could you add to your own power word list below? And don't forget to add to this list when you come across new, relevant words.

Write for your boss

It's true you do need to check how bosses expect you to write. Look at their writing. Is there a generational style; a corporate house style? Beyond that, do people write differently for each target audience? Tune in.

Analyse why you've been hired. Was it because you are tech-savvy and/or you're buzzing with ideas? In that case, managers might really appreciate you offering constructive suggestions if you feel the writing there is outmoded or simply doesn't work as it should.

So, how could your writing actually help improve things? Streamlining communication could be a quick win. Busy bosses dread information overload: people constantly seeking direction and copying them in unnecessarily to lengthy, disordered missives. They're too busy to sift through data. Conversely, they also hate having too little information to make informed decisions.

Meeting notes/minutes – structure them to impress

Here's a useful example of everyday business writing. A manager asks an employee how they plan to write up the minutes of a meeting held that day. The employee emails back:

> I'll be recording what everyone says and then writing this up afterwards, for circulation to all who attended. I hope you find this helpful.

That's certainly concise writing but it's not effective. How much more helpful to the manager would be a considered, structured response along these lines:

> I propose to:
>
> – write up all material points
> – indicate what items were closed (needing no further action)
> – indicate what actions are ongoing, and who does what, when
> – write an action plan and ensure everyone who needs to know does – which may be more than just the people who attended the meeting

And what do you know, now we have an easy and winning format for meeting notes and minutes! Understand your strengths in thinking through the brief; your ideas, your disruptiveness (in the sense of innovating change for the better!) and write with structured points aimed at producing a good end result. It's a habit you can easily slip into.

Reports – your checklist for success

Report writing is another key writing task, so let me help you impress your boss. As far as you can, identify before you write:

• Why are you writing and who will be your key readers?
• How much do they know?

- Do they need to use the report? If so, how? For example, to improve results in areas in which they are accountable? To be kept informed about others' achievements?

- Are they interested in the report – or must you create that interest?

- Must you inform/persuade/cover yourself/anticipate problems/ offer solutions?

- Do you need to monitor any results and have an ongoing status record?

A checklist to help you plan

- Take time to understand the brief and evaluate the business case.

- Ascertain the deadline.

- Who has input alongside yours (if anyone)?

- Check and set the relevant background.

- Understand the target audience and how to write for them.

- What analysis is needed?

- What recommendations should you or others make?

- Draw up your plan.

- Write the report and evaluate how to make the right impact, distinguishing between:

  - the 'essential to know'

  - the 'nice to know'

  - the 'don't need to know'

- Check what you have written for both sense and logic.

- Check your writing for mistakes in your English, including a spellcheck and grammar check in the correct variety of English.

- Issue and check both the outcomes and the feedback after your audience has received your report or review.

Understand your strengths and appreciate what your boss needs

By now you'll be getting a clearer picture of the way forward and the following case study provides an illustration that brings the issue to life.

CASE STUDY   Bringing people along on the journey

Here's a real-life email exchange from a boss in a major international company to a junior member of staff, recruited a couple of months before:

> **Boss:** So, how's it going? What's the dream?
>
> **Employee:** To have lots of data.
>
> **Boss:** Oh, that sounds like a nightmare to me. What are you going to do with the data?
>
> **Employee:** That's a tricky one. I'm going to have to go away and think about that.

The very next week she emailed over:

> **Employee:** I've analysed the data so far and we need to drive results in... (she then highlighted a specific area).

She had cut through the noise, as requested, to deliver positive action.

She was pleased and her boss was pleased. The communication exchange had worked for both. The boss had motivated the employee by highlighting her expertise, admitting that was not his skill set. He guided her by highlighting how to focus. He needed data not just to produce information but to gain knowledge on which to build results. Together they delivered. That's how you bring people along on the journey via writing effectively.

When you're the boss, writing brings extra challenges!

Accessible, inclusive language that says the right things brings people on board, as we saw in the Nationwide case study. Time after time, simple can be smart. It's easy for each of us to forget that! It's definitely time to ditch any 'I'm cleverer than you' obfuscation. I'm using the inaccessible-to-many word *obfuscation* to make a point. Your business English is not clever if people don't readily understand it, across cultures and generations.

As a boss, you're at the stage of your career where you should know that confusing and reader-unfriendly messages can = lost profits + lost sales and/or custom + loss of professionalism + lost goodwill. Beyond this, you need to be credible so people will trust what you say and what you do.

You also need to:

- inspire and grow your people
- encourage ideas and interaction
- identify talent and strengths, develop teams accordingly
- listen and learn
- communicate values and strategy
- persuade – and get great results
- know how to communicate good and bad news effectively

It's a tall order!

It's taken time and effort recruiting, you've got to see it through: your employees need to see writing that makes them feel valued, through the good times and the bad.

Make the workplace as enjoyable an experience as you can. Deliver the promise you made when you attracted them. In terms of your business writing, check your messages align with their goals alongside yours. Writing becomes more about the 'we' than simply the 'I'. You'll find you get people on board much more easily by reframing (as just one example) 'You must do this' to 'We all need this to work because...' and give the reasons why such action must happen.

Have you got a corporate writing style guide in place? Should you? This is a brave new business world we're entering and you ignore the importance of written word power at your peril!

Spontaneous positive emails from bosses can act as a figurative pat on the back, such as:

> 'That was a job well done. Keep up the good work.'

> 'You made great use of your strong negotiating skills there!'

> 'I'm delighted to report to shareholders that it's the teams' consistent efforts during difficult trading conditions that have brought about these improved results.'

This writing can really bolster morale and make employees feel valued. As I've mentioned before, it removes an element of what's increasingly classed as 'toxicity in the workplace'.

If something has not gone so well, a timely email from a manager can still be viewed positively by employees, for example:

> 'Yes, that was a tricky scenario – one to learn from another time. If something like it arises again, it could be ideal to contact [name of colleague with experience] for their advice.'

This latter example demonstrates the manager's empathy for the difficult situation the employee has faced and also offers positive guidance on a likely solution for next time.

Stay up to date. Check that the voice and tone of your writing also aligns with the other channels the organization uses. It's never a good idea, as a boss, to become a 'communication dinosaur' because *you* don't listen and learn too. It doesn't mean you have to go the other extreme though, with overly casual sentences, such as:

> 'Why did you do that, huh?'

> 'Get with the power words, pal!'

'Gravitas' matters: it signifies the respect earned by serious intelligence. It's a power word one 20-something client identified to me as being an essential characteristic in a boss. I agree that managers' writing needs to show both gravitas and authority, to earn staff's respect and trust in what the managers are communicating. If you are to lead, people need to know why they should follow, and why being proactive will take everyone forward. Effective writing helps do just that.

Writing across generations in your customer base

The tips I have given so far will help you write successfully across your multigenerational client base too. One style of writing won't suit all. Look at how your target audience writes, not just in cultural terms but in generational terms too, and mirror it as far as is valid to do so, without losing your professional authenticity.

Your checklist for action

- Keep up to date with what today's business writing 'looks and feels like' – to create the best reader experience you can.

- Develop writing skills that will boost your marketability at every stage of your career.

- Write accessibly (at every level, as shown in this chapter) and consistently communicate your and your organization's values.

- 'Write the talk' as consistently as you can, even in technical writing.

- Enjoy identifying and using power words that work for you and your readers, to engage, energize and persuade.

- Plan and structure *all* your writing – not just your meeting notes, minutes and reports.

- Understand how to draw the main points out of the detail.

- Write courteously, and as positively and supportively as possible.

- Keep people in the loop.
- Write to connect with your customers and wider audiences; this will also involve embracing diversity in all its forms, including generations, and pulling departments, disciplines and teams together.
- Write with authority as well as authenticity.

References

BBC (2020) *Jonathan Van-Tam's best analogies: Penalties, equalizers and yoghurts*, www.bbc.co.uk/news/uk-55169801 (archived at https://perma.cc/ZN36-AYAW)

Octopus Energy (nd) Doing things differently, from 'Love & Power' to the Wheel of Fortune [blog], octopus.energy/blog/why-we-do-things-differently-from-love-power-to-the-wheel-of-fortune/ (archived at https://perma.cc/Y7YD-CCBR)

04
Quality matters

Top quality? Or medium? Or low? What bar will you set for yourself and your readers?

What does quality mean to you?

Let's say you've bought a new coat and you find it's got a flaw in it when you get home. Or you follow the washing instructions on your new sweater but find they were faulty, and your sweater has shrunk as a result!

Or maybe that pack of chocolate biscuits from supplier B is clearly of lesser quality than those from supplier A, although the price is just about the same. Or the presentation of that gift you were thinking of buying is messy and unprofessional-looking. So you buy from someone else.

In all these cases you'll be making a decision about what quality means to you – and which supplier you will stay with, and which you may complain to, or tell others about your disappointing experience.

Well, all these considerations can be applied to how our readers may judge your writing, and let's not forget, this also can ultimately mean brand you!

Ultimately it's up to you – and your organization – to define what you mean by *quality* business writing. Does it mean 'top quality' or simply acceptable, both from your and your readers' perspectives? This squares with one aspect of Step 1 on the ladder of success in Chapter 2.

Make an honest appraisal!

How do you want to be seen? What do you want to be remembered for? To be professional, it's best to get your business English writing right, first time and every time. Let's reinforce the points made so far:

- Each bit of business writing you send out can be (indeed should be) viewed as an advertisement for 'brand you' (which I'll explain below), as well as for your company.

- Written words can be 'frozen' at the point in time when we first wrote them. They are judged for what they are when we are not there to explain them.

- They have to be the right words for your commercial purpose and from your readers' perspective.

And what a missed opportunity if you don't write to impress: to be the best you can. Don't settle for less; the competition won't!

'Brand you'

It may be that you have never thought of yourself as a brand. But it can help your career greatly to understand that your personal brand can emerge when you think along these lines:

- Why not commit to delivering the best you can by 'being you'?

- Seize the opportunity of what 'bringing you' to the table brings: a difference for the better.

- Let people see that in everything you write, you come over as strongly as your organization.

- By doing this you become valuable to your valued reader.

- From the start readers can feel warm rather than cold towards your suggestions.

- As your career progresses, you will be able to further identify and strengthen what has emerged as 'brand you'.

We all make mistakes, don't we?

Well, yes. Whatever our proficiency in a language, we're all likely to make written mistakes sometimes. A tip that really works is: expect to find mistakes at the important draft stage. This is an essential stage in what we could call the three stages of writing:

1 plan

2 draft

3 issue

That way you're more likely to:

- spot mistakes at draft stage
- remove them before sending writing out
- present a totally professional corporate image

Yes, checking, even double-checking, your writing before you send it does take more time. But it's an investment in quality that pays great dividends. Congratulations if it's second nature to you! It's not the case for everyone. This is particularly true in high-pressure environments where, sadly, it's rare to say 'slow down' – even though speed can foster mistakes, which actually take up even more time to resolve.

Written mistakes come in many forms

They can be as simple as:

- 'Your welcome' instead of the correct grammar: 'You're welcome'.
- 'Defiantly' instead of the correct spelling: 'definitely' (and what a difference in meaning this makes!).
- 'Were is the meeting?' instead of 'Where is the meeting?'.

I'm deliberately using expressions that people get wrong time and time again. There'll be others that occur to you. As you'll know, some can cause unintended amusement, some will produce eyerolls, some offence.

But mistakes aren't just about punctuation and grammar and so on. Let's look at two problematic sentences. Try to predict how readers might react.

1. Thank you for your order. You are demanded to send payment within 30 days.

Firstly, the expression 'you are demanded' isn't correct English. It's better to write something on the lines of 'Please send payment within 30 days' or 'You are requested to pay within 30 days'. The expression 'to demand payment' has a very strong connotation. It's generally used for the final notice before a company pursues legal action, to collect money owing to it in an overdue account. When the expression is used validly, it would be on the following lines: 'This is a final demand for payment (within 30 days) of your outstanding account.'

So in our first example we have an outright grammatical mistake. But the wrong tone can also count as a writing mistake.

Let's look at the text again: 'Thank you for your order. You are demanded to send payment within 30 days.' Although the reader sees the initial words 'Thank you', the next sentence introduces a harsh, accusatory tone. Yet this is clearly one of the first points of contact between customer and company. The order has just been placed: 'Thank you for your order' tells us that. Is the customer going to feel that this is a nice company to do business with? I don't think so.

When new customers make orders, you should make this a very positive experience for them. If a company can't be bothered to write well here, the indicators are not good for future business success. Customers usually have a choice: there is likely to be an alternative company that they like to do business with. Which would you choose?

Let's take a look at another example of a written mistake.

2. We can certainly provide the services you request in principal.

Homonyms are words that have the same or similar sound and sometimes the same spelling as another, but whose meanings are different (more on this in Chapter 9). But let's just take a look here at two words that are frequently confused by native and non-native English writers alike. They are:

principal: an adjective generally meaning first in importance; also a noun meaning a chief or senior person, or an original sum of money for investment

principle: a noun meaning a fundamental truth or quality; a rule or belief governing a person's morally correct behaviour and attitudes

In the second example, unfortunately the writer has chosen the wrong version of the homonym. The correct word would be 'principle'. Some readers may not mind this; some will not notice. But some will make a value judgement: this is wrong!

It may be unfair but just *one wrong word* can undermine readers' perception of a writer's or a company's professionalism. It can also distract readers' attention away from the writer's key message.

Although I've just highlighted some mistakes, I'm definitely not suggesting a 'red pen' approach. Some managers used to use a red pen (or now a digital editing equivalent) to highlight an employee's written mistakes. It's horribly unsupportive across the board, to native and non-native English speakers alike. It's also particularly unfair to dyslexic or other neurodiverse employees and can really demotivate staff. Helpful suggestions work much better.

It's true that sometimes you just have to write the way your line manager suggests. But it's always better to know the reasons why they consider one way better than another. Even in UK English you can write certain words in two ways, both of which are correct. You can write 'recognize' or 'recognise', or 'judgement' or 'judgment' – and it can be personal or company preference that dictates which you use. If you don't understand the reasons why you must write a certain way, your manager owes it to you to explain why. You also owe it to yourself to ask why!

It's in your own interest to know if you make mistakes. Problems do occur and every business needs to identify them. How else can we seek solutions and get things right?

Activity

Are there any 'quality' issues that you have come across in business writing? Why was that? Why not jot ones that come to mind here.

How did they make you or other readers feel? Unimpressed? Confused? Embarrassed, either for yourself or for your business? Irritated – even angry?

....

....

....

....

....

Further costs of getting your writing wrong

We've seen earlier how things can go wrong when we don't update written messages in the light of changed circumstances. The following scenario also shows other costs businesses can pay for getting writing wrong.

I submitted a database entry on my business to a company for inclusion in a Europe-wide guide. Their fee seemed reasonable, given the likely exposure to new business. I had to follow their format with limited word count, so my entry was as in the box below.

TQI Word Power Skills training

Activity: A UK company that provides business support services for every type of business. It provides Business English services to help with marketing literature and communication skills training.

Services include editing, text correction or fine tuning, quality assurance, proofreading, group workshops, individual coaching in Business English and cross-cultural briefing.

These innovative, fully confidential business services are designed to help you assure the quality of your service or product and help you hit your commercial target first and every time.

TQI Word Power Skills training offers businesses of all types and sizes expert and affordable solutions for their Business English needs, together with international experience from previous consultancy in the Netherlands.

Co-operation request: TQI Word Power Skills training seeks companies requiring these services.

A few weeks later I received an invoice from the company concerned. Attached to this was a copy of the entry as it had actually appeared. Unknown to me, the copy had already gone live, Europe-wide, one month before I received the invoice. The entry was now the one shown below. It includes a number of errors, made when the company inputted my original wording onto the database. Can you spot these mistakes?

TQI Word Power Skills training

Activity: UK company that provides business support services for every type of business, it provides Business english services to help with marketing literature and communication skills training.

Services include editing, text correction or fine tuning, quality assurance, proof reading, group workshops, infivudal coaching in Business English and cross cultural breifing.

These Innovative fully confidential business services are designed to help you assure the quality of your service or product and help you hit your commercial target first and every time.

TQI Word Power Skills training offers businesses of all types and sizes expert and affordable solutions for their business English needs, international expereince from previous consultancy in the Netherland.

Co-operation request: TQI Word Power Skills training seeks companies that require there servces.

Understandably, I wasn't at all happy, especially when presented with an invoice to pay for this appalling entry. Can you see why? Look closely and you'll see at least one mistake in each paragraph. Some are spelling mistakes, such as 'infivdual' for 'individual', 'briefing' for 'briefing' and 'expereince' for 'experience', 'cross cultural' for 'cross-cultural' and 'english' for 'English'. Some are inconsistencies, such as 'business English' and 'Business English'. Both may be used, but it's better style to keep to a single use, certainly within one paragraph. The word innovative suddenly has a capital 'I', thus we find 'Innovative' even though the word is mid-sentence. There are other mistakes too. One thing's sure: nobody ran a spell-check or grammar check.

What ultimately was the cost of this regrettable incident? Well, it might surprise you that there was an actual cost to pay on as many as five different levels! You see:

1 I refused to pay the invoice because the entry was incorrect, so the company suffered the loss of that income.

2 That company then had to redraft a correct entry, which cost them duplication of work.

3 They then had to make arrangements to replace the incorrect entry at another time, at their own further cost.

4 One cost to my company was in terms of seriously undermined professional credibility and reputation (both short and long term).

5 I also paid a price in losing the publicity timeslot I had requested. A later entry was not ideal for my business purpose.

Can you see how such an apparently low-key set of mistakes can have a disastrous effect on the professional credibility and reputation of a company?

In the final analysis, the mistakes weren't mine, but they *appeared* to be mine. It was my company name and my details that appeared… which leads me to the next section.

You can never fully outsource your writing

What that last episode taught me was this: not to assume that because the version I sent for publishing was correct, the published version would be correct too. The advertising company used different technology. They didn't just copy and paste from my original digital file: they retyped the copy themselves. Whether or not this was the case, I should have asked to see the final proof before publication. Printers often provide this as a matter of course, to cover themselves against complaints at a later stage. But note that word 'often' – it's not the same as 'always'!

If you outsource something and it goes wrong, the backlash becomes yours too. You can't outsource responsibility!

Proofreading tips

Check everything you write before you send it out. Expect mistakes. Tips to help are:

- Allow sufficient time for proofreading. If you rush, you may still overlook the mistakes you are looking for.

- It's easier to proofread on paper than on screen (though be eco-friendly about this).

- Use a standard or online dictionary or grammar book to help you, or your computer's spelling and grammar check (set on the correct variant of English for your target audience). Remember this is not fail-safe. It may let the wrong word(s) through, especially homonyms, for example 'brake' for 'break', 'there' for 'their' and so on.

- Watch out for autocorrect wrongly changing your correct words such as 'its' to 'it's' or 'definitely' to 'defiantly'.

- Try reading your lines backwards (people sometimes use a ruler to read one line at a time, to avoid distraction). You don't check meaning this way, but you can check the words are written correctly.

- Now check for meaning and logic.

- Make a self-help list of any words you regularly get wrong, so that you can check them quickly and effectively next time you write them.

Your checklist for action

- Set the bar – preferably aim for top quality!

- Understand that mistakes can always happen.

- Take steps to minimize this, such as running spellcheck and grammar check in the right variety of English.

- Realize mistakes aren't just about spelling and grammar. They can also be when words are left out, when sentences confuse, or facts are presented in a disorderly way that might even distort the correct message.

- Understand the longer-term impact mistakes may have (and how these can in turn impact on you and your company). Highlight this to others.

- Do an overall check of your writing before you issue it.

- If you're unsure of something, ask for help from someone who will know.

05
Telling your story through social media

Balancing broadcasting with conversation; linking your story with your readers' stories.

Social media has shaken 'the rules' of business writing

Just as the printing press revolutionized the way written communication could spread messages far and wide, so social media has turned the business world and traditional writing inside out.

Let's immerse ourselves in the fuller picture to see how the social media 'storyline' fits together, integrating broadcasting and conversation.

Get into the social media mindset

From the simple sharing of a message to in-depth conversation, to following the latest news, to opening transactions and closing deals, social media is an intrinsic part of our world. Once again written words feature strongly. What you need to write depends on your personal and company story, the points you want to make, the goals you need to achieve, and how you write to attract and maintain readers' interaction with you, as the story evolves.

Get your business message to anyone, anywhere, anytime

It's all about sharing information and collaborating online, bringing the facility to enable everyone to get in touch with anyone, anywhere, anytime. In business, although the biggest players have the biggest budget, they can't get complacent. Even the smallest voice now has a megaphone to communicate globally, be part of the conversation – and go viral. So how do we set about it?

Visuals are hugely important – but it's captions that can sell

High resolution visuals yield impact and are a huge feature in today's business communication. But arguably written content remains king. It's rare for even the best visuals to work by themselves: it's usually the captions and descriptions and written follow-up that ultimately sell the messages. Infographics can be immensely valuable, almost at a glance, via thought-through visuals aided by writing that imparts key information interestingly and concisely. But they're costly to produce and currently there's a move towards stand-alone graphics with minimal text.

So it's crucial for this text to be on point: relevant to the optics, relevant to the business purpose and leading to the required action.

If you want to draw in a deal of thousands of dollars of business, is your three-line caption going to be the best way to secure it, on its own? Maybe not, but make it link to further enticing information and that could seal the deal.

And if we look at rather less exotic transactions, such as online selling of everyday items, what do we see? Read the following case study to find out.

CASE STUDY   Powerful descriptions sell

Some practical examples are to be found in the world of online auctions – arguably some of the earliest sites on social media platforms.

Let's say two separate sellers each have one of two identical, brand new, specialized category CDs to sell:

- Seller 1 shows the picture of the CD and simply lists the CD's title (and spells it wrongly) and names the asking price.

- Seller 2 shows the same picture, writes the title correctly, stresses how it's *brand new* and one of the most acclaimed CDs of the year in its category.

Seller 2 is *creating interest* – and at the same time setting out the information in an accurate, professional way. This seller also asks a higher price than seller 1.

You may think that the lower price will win every time – but it's not always the case. On occasion the one with 'power wording' (seller 2) can sell for double the price. The more expensive the product, the greater this effect can be. People will often pay a premium for (perceived) quality.

Even when it comes to selling and buying larger specialist items, you might be surprised how writing can make all the difference. A written description may be the most important aspect a potential buyer has to focus on. As an illustration, imagine you are selling a power generator online. Your potential buyer is not going to be able to try it out. There may not be a review they can go on. They have narrowed it down to two models: yours and a competitor's. The pictures of the two models are very similar. It's possible they have been manufactured in the same factory under different marques. Yet the price difference between the two could be 200 per cent.

Seller 1 has posted the picture and the price. Seller 2 has also added descriptive power words such as 'state of the art', 'reliable' and 'guaranteed'. Once again, a dynamic powerful description adds value in making the product stand out, engage interest and – very importantly – sell.

And never lose sight of the fact that you need regularly to *express* your USP (unique selling point/proposition) where your readers will catch sight of it. Make it punchy in the first instance, make it compelling in the longer term.

Activity

You're almost sure to have had some engagement with online auction sites at some stage, either as a seller or buyer. And you might not have realized how much the written part matters.

So now do get into the habit of noting the sort of writing that attracts your attention and makes you want to buy. Conversely what sort of writing has the exact opposite effect? Take the opportunity of jotting down your findings here.

Refresh content, update details

People constantly check their networks, so update content. Keep people posted on things such as helpful information, breaking news, innovation, events, offers, etc.

Written content also needs to be suitable for mobile devices and smart watches. Users who are 'on the go', maybe waiting for a train or between meetings, need easily highlighted messages and to know at a glance where you're leading. The original 'click here' has given way to the (hopefully) more enticing 'read more'.

We see social media used alongside, sometimes in place of, traditional leaflets or mailing. Being social offers the opportunity (and expectation) to talk not just about brand, products and services but also to introduce personalities: the people behind the brand. There's more opportunity for storytelling that resonates and a huge demand for customized messages to elicit buy-in or positive reaction. The Word Power Skills system shown in Chapter 2 is immensely valuable, as the challenge (and the exciting part) is how to get your words heard through the noise. How to adapt, to keep up with the trends – and even create them.

How is English used across platforms?

English has such an advantage, being used extensively across multiple platforms. But if English isn't your company's first language or that of your social media writers, be mindful that words that are right for your home market may not work abroad, even where English is the common language.

As an example, let's look at this wording that impressed me some time ago on sportswear brand Adidas' global website:

> Go get better, share your skills, compare yourself with the best and challenge your friends.

It used very clear wording, easily understandable on first reading. Let's contrast this with wording used on their Adidas India website at that time:

> Criticism and self-doubt can paralyse the most talented athletes. Only a rare breed converts the stones thrown at them into milestones...

The language is rather more poetic and thought-provoking. It requires a more sophisticated understanding of the English used.

Coca-Cola is one of the most recognized global brands and it too adapts the English it uses across the world. So although the social media hashtag #PerfectCoke worked globally, some countries won't necessarily have understood #SwelterStopper used for ice-cool Coke or #SarapNgFirst – 'the first time taste of the

#PerfectCoke experience'. This latter example purposefully features Tagalog English to resonate with their target youth market in the Philippines.

Using a digital agency? You can't outsource responsibility!

If you decide to outsource any of your social media (especially likely if you export), or if you simply collaborate with other partners, don't forget you're ultimately accountable for the messages you put out. One charity, Samaritans, found this out to their cost, despite their best intentions.

CASE STUDY   Samaritans

Samaritans is a highly respected UK charity, offering support to anyone in emotional distress.

Looking for ways of helping vulnerable people online (especially those aged 18 to 35), the charity hired a digital agency to help it launch the #SamaritansRadar app. This sent an alert to users when people they followed posted messages that algorithms picked up to suggest depressed or suicidal thoughts.

The app was withdrawn almost immediately after attracting criticism that it didn't work. It certainly failed on a semantic level, as one Twitter user showed. He added the #SamaritansRadar hashtag to his innocuous post: 'Making a mixtape of smooth jazz classics. Maybe I should end it all with a bit of Alfonzo Blackwell. #SamaritansRadar.'

The algorithm had mistakenly picked up on the words 'maybe I should end it all' as alluding to suicide.

What are the key objectives?

These include: engage, be shared and convert – by being relevant, useful, knowledgeable, credible, consistently professional and personable.

It's not in the scope of this book to cover writing for websites or search engine optimization (SEO) in any detail. But it's important to know that the algorithms of Google and other search engines look out for certain signals (that may change over time). Your focus always has to be about creating good-quality content and coherence between your website and your communication off that platform, including social media posts. How engaging both are affects your visibility and could impact on your SEO ranking. Google's guidelines for SEO state that pages must be written primarily for users, not for search engines: '#1: Focus on the user and all else will follow' and this rings true for social media generally.

Beyond that you will need:

- a clear structure that's easy to read
- useful links that add value to the text (that is, don't link for the sake of it)
- to engage social signals that are likely to improve your visibility

'Social signals' are the interactions your website and social media posts are gaining (visits, likes, shares, dialogue, etc). It's important to realize that you're no longer just broadcasting, you need to be part of a conversation – and a listener too. When everyone is an author, make sure you're generating content that's valued. Write things of interest, offer value, project a brand that engages, get involved – and show you're interested too.

Look at this Facebook offer from Pizza Express (fast-food company) in the following case study.

CASE STUDY   Create your new favourite pizza

Pizza Express posted a Facebook offer, inviting diners to join them in celebrating their new Spring menu. Their enticement was: 'Create your own pizza to feature on our Autumn menu.'

The winning pizza would join the favourites on their menu and '£10,000 AND a holiday for two to the Amalfi Coast could all be yours!'.

Emblazoned at the side of the page was: 'Free Dough Balls for every entry!', i.e. every entrant is actually a winner.

The success of the offer is in the result and they were instantly eliciting positive interaction, such as: 'Thanks/Cheers/BIG THANKS!!/A fairly amazing prize bundle, and a fun competition too! They've done a really nice job with that competition...'.

Let's analyse the components of their successful writing:

1 There was a compelling headline that appealed to the individual reader.

2 There was a great offer – not just the chance of the 'fairly amazing prize bundle' as one reader put it, but also a freebie for every entrant.

3 For discoverability, the tags were 'holiday' and 'Pizza Express'.

4 There was also a link to their website and Pizza Express deals.

Look out for examples for yourself. See what you feel works, and you're sure to find writing that:

- expresses key messages in the right channel, in language that's right for the expectations, needs, aspirations and interests of the target audience on that platform (casual/more formal/culture/ right for that generation, etc?)

- has compelling headlines that attract target readers' attention (more on this shortly)

- communicates even complex messages simply (links can take readers to detail needed)
- maintains interest and credibility (readers must trust you to know links will take them to something professional/of value, otherwise why click?)
- is current or refreshed useful content

Your business objectives are usually any or all of the following:

- to increase brand awareness and 'be part of a conversation' (as positively as possible)
- to get your messages across and, depending on your business, to boost sales
- to create ongoing dialogue, listen to customers and improve
- to gain market insights
- to share valuable information, develop and maintain relationships
- to get your messages found widely through SEO

Keep up with the major platforms out there

Businesses need to choose the channels that best suit their needs – and also those of their target demographic. Current leaders include Instagram, Facebook, YouTube, WhatsApp, TikTok, Pinterest, Snapchat, WeChat, Reddit, Twitter and LinkedIn. Keep up to date, as platforms constantly change. As more channels get added to the mix, recognize and adapt to their style. Keep *your purpose in mind* and be clear.

Then, you can't just expect everyone to open, let's say, a Facebook or Twitter account in order to engage with you. Choose channels you know your audience is interested in too and remember that not everyone wants to be on the same channel. For example, upcoming generations don't usually want to be on the same platform as their elders! Be prepared to invest time in getting social, otherwise how can you expect to create a loyal following or generate leads?

How do companies shine through their social media interaction?

Firstly, they get to know which channels are business-to-business (B2B) like LinkedIn (who help businesses to network but not directly sell), which are direct-to-consumer (D2C) and can actively sell, and which mix the two. This knowledge dictates how they must write. In all cases, it's about sharing information and experiences of value, the newest this, the helpful that, etc. If people value a company's content, they can become 'brand advocates' remotely.

The next case study highlights how one highly successful entrepreneur maintains his standing as a major player in social media.

CASE STUDY   Steven Bartlett: social media influencer

Steven Bartlett is a speaker, investor, author, content creator and the host of one of Europe's biggest podcasts, *The Diary of a CEO*. He has shot to fame while still in his twenties, initially as the founder of Social Chain, which became one of the world's most influential social media companies.

Described as one of Europe's most accomplished young entrepreneurs and philosophical thinkers, his profile has been further widened on BBC TV's *Dragon's Den*. Budding entrepreneurs get three minutes to pitch their business ideas to five multimillionaires, who are willing to invest cash, time and expertise to kick-start the business.

So how does he communicate so successfully on social media channels? What tips can we glean?

Let's look first at his Instagram account, with 2 million followers. We can see that his posts often start as broadcasting, and that he varies his posts. Sometimes he starts with high resolution photos, accompanied by captions. These lead into video interviews. Sometimes the posts are simply motivational written messages.

In all cases, we soon find followers' replies flood in. Now we can see how 'broadcasting' morphs into 'conversation' – the true purpose of social media. The replies he garners are generally upbeat, as he knows how to reach his intended audience positively. He uses *their language* to strike a chord and inspire, which is his stated aim here.

If we look at the engagement metrics, it may surprise you to find that the written posts can garner more likes and comments than the videos. As one example, an Instagram post, 'seven things most people take a lifetime to learn', at the time of writing had garnered over 160,000 likes. To give you a flavour, the seventh thing he mentioned was:

> The world starts and ends entirely inside your mind. No matter where you end up, no matter how rich or successful you become, you won't enjoy any of it if you get there at the expense of your mental health.

At the end of the list he wrote: 'What would you add?' and drew in 869 suggestions.

Now let's look at one of his tweets under the handle @SteveBartlettSC that's particularly interesting in terms of the remit of this book. It precedes a link to his YouTube interview with Greg Hoffman, *The Marketing Genius Behind Nike* (part of his *Diary of a CEO* series). It reads:

> If you own a business, work for a brand or are getting to grips with marketing this is a must watch.

> Greg's knowledge, experience and wisdom in this area is second to none.

> You probably want a pen and paper for this one… trust me.

> WATCH NOW.

On another occasion, when he live-tweeted during the showing of an episode of *Dragon's Den*, a swift reply was: 'I love that you're watching and tweeting with the rest of us.'

This is a very apt observation on the inclusivity he fosters, as simply as this. And it's a very useful phenomenon for us all. If you've attended successful social events, you'll know how live-tweeting can amplify the feelgood factor: 'it's great, we're in it together, let's share with others!' In the business world, it's no different. A huge inclusive buzz can be created by attendees at conferences, for example, live-tweeting facts and observations following high-profile speakers' talks or presentations. Once again, broadcasting can very effectively spill over into 'written conversation'. Clearly the more positive this is, the better from a business perspective. No surprise there!

In another live-tweeting exchange, a follower noticed that one of the older Dragons in the programme was keen to tap into Steven's expertise in social media. They posed an interesting comment: 'Age issue or just simply behind on social media power?'

And if the explanation as to why people aren't social media savvy is 'it's an age issue' or 'simply behind on social media power', it's even more reason for companies to pool all generations' strengths. You know how strongly I'm encouraging this throughout the book.

Have you come across Steven Bartlett's posts? Or are there other social media influencers you actively and positively respond to? Why is that? Do get in the habit of analysing their technique, so that you can use winning methods yourself.

Here's how I see it:

- Broadcasting becomes even more meaningful and results-based when it turns into conversation.

- This is how you bring people along – both on your journey and their own life journey.

- Posts interrelate life values alongside business interests, in tune with today's world.

- If posts are interesting enough, they create an appetite for more – so you need to update your content frequently, both to retain and extend your following

- Where Steven makes the point that 'you probably want paper and pen for this one' he's expressing a clear belief in the written word.

- There are various schools of thought on the power of committing things to writing. In terms of aspiration, many believe that if you write your aspirations down, you focus more clearly on achieving them. I'm also suggesting that writing helps you plan your action.

- Beyond this, it's often inferred that writing affords greater recall for points that are important for the reader to revisit.

- Interestingly, the 'words of wisdom' written quotes often gain more replies than the videos.

- Steven's website further highlights his belief in the written word providing lasting influence, providing a link to his best-selling book *Happy Sexy Millionaire*.

Writing that creates trust can create a community

Steven Bartlett is building a following in his targeted demographic, inspired by his content. Encouragingly, we are seeing more companies who want to use their profits for the public good.

Charismatic retail magnate Theo Paphitis is also keen to support his followers and he targets a very specific entrepreneurial readership. As a retailer, he fosters a community that is more business-to-business (B2B) focused, as the following case study shows.

CASE STUDY   Theo Paphitis' Small Business Sunday community

In common with many highly successful entrepreneurs, Theo Paphitis is open about his dyslexia, which has actually afforded him an advantage in understanding the importance of simple, vibrant, well-chosen words to sell messages, products and services and create a following.

He realized how helpful it would be to small businesses in the UK (known to be the lifeblood of the economy) to understand that writing with impact on social media was a powerful tool for networking and growth.

To this end, he created Small Business Sunday (shortened to the hashtag #SBS on Twitter). Each week, he rewards small businesses that tweet him @TheoPaphitis and write about their businesses in one tweet (with hashtag #SBS) in a dedicated time slot, on a Sunday. He then retweets his favourite lucky six, judged on how well they have communicated their message. As he has over 493,000 followers, this provides them with a massive publicity boost.

Theo continues to build this #SBS community with offers and events for winners, but also by providing interaction within the community itself. He and his group of companies actively get involved in the conversation.

In his words:

> My vision is that everyone who has ever won an #SBS retweet from me becomes part of a friendly club. Like-minded individuals can share successes and learnings... I know I have been lucky in business and I am keen now to spread goodwill to others, of course not forgetting that very often you make your own luck by making use of every opportunity.

This and similar cases are exciting applications of business writing in today's workplace. Can you see how, where English is a common language, such skilful use of social media to build communities can be rolled out – not simply on a local basis but nationally and internationally too? We saw in Chapter 3 how strongly upcoming generations feel about 'putting something back' into the world. It's a great trend for all to embrace.

Discoverability with added value

It's not just short posts that can go viral. Now 'everyone is a writer' – but not everyone is willing or able to write good material in depth. Articles with detailed information can be highly valuable.

'Digital storytelling' has become a big focus of online marketing and aims at encouraging user-generated content (UGC) which the two preceding case studies demonstrate. Naturally you must write the right information so people find your posts. Without discoverability, you won't get shared! So provide the right links, photos, etc.

Your stories can be brief but sometimes it's the detail that makes them come alive as I'll continue to show in this chapter. That's the beauty of being able to provide a link in your short post to a fuller article on your website or elsewhere.

As part of the story, consider intriguing your readers – maybe hold some information back, so they want to explore further. A link can take them to that valuable 'more'. But avoid 'clickbait' – the pejorative term to describe captivating links that only take you to spam advertisements etc.

The important thing is that all your posts work towards a common goal. Are you going to post similar material across the platforms you use? Whatever you do, the messages need to harmonize.

Further writing tips for key channels

General tips

Channels will continue to change or even disappear as we have seen with early ones such as Friends Reunited, MySpace and, more recently, the changed ownership of Twitter. Tips that I gave in earlier editions of this book will continue to have currency on existing and future channels. The principles usefully stand the test of time.

So let me add some more here:

- Algorithms help ensure that content that's helpful gets found and shared. So write tips/hacks on things that work or problems to avoid, inspirational quotes, universal truths or something relating to a trending topic, etc.

- You can actively ask people to share your information: 'please share' or 'please retweet' can work for good content.

- Analyse which posts are popular.

- Post in the right time zone for your potential global readers. Social media is fast-moving and transient, so re-post tweaked items at differing intervals – and double-check for mistakes before you post. Speed can trap you into making them!

- Hashtags are useful for introducing topics of general interest and are searchable, for example #BusinessCommunication or #globalprojects.

Where writers err is when the message is all about *them* and nothing to do with others. What do you think of this tweet sent to me?

> Hey what do you do? I deliver strategic digital transformation. Come over and like my Facebook page!

If you have written a good bio, complete with your website details, any writer should have the courtesy to read the outline of what you do, before making contact in this way. This tweet is actually only about them. And would you talk to this person so directly, without introduction or further evidence, in any other business situation? Also, they can't assume the reader will be on Facebook.

As social media is about writing for people, not robots – and will continue to be, even in an age of increasing artificial intelligence

(AI) – it requires accessible, conversational language. I think post 2 below generally works better for the medium than post 1:

1 There's little doubt about it, it feels rather good that my business writing book appears to be useful as it's selling.

2 Woohoo, so pleased: my book is in the #businesswriting charts because it helps! Thank you so much! #lovemyreaders.

But if the style is too effusive for your target audience, don't use it. Use your judgement – and, as I mention throughout, it's a must to have a policy on language that's off limits, e.g. expletives or religious/political/sexist/racist comments.

Remember also that people use social media to make immediate complaints. If your company is involved, be sure to monitor for them and deal with them quickly. Others will be watching how you deal with this too.

Facebook

Facebook is currently the world's largest social networking site and so offers enormous potential for going viral. You may consider this a strong case for using global rather than local English (see Chapter 7).

When writing a company Facebook page, create relationships with users. Show you are there to do business with them. Be interesting; offer something to attract visitors to your page and get them to hit 'Like' – a visible approval of a product or service.

Writing tips to help are:

- Be authentic, let readers see your personality, on a professional basis.

- Keep personal comments for your personal accounts, have a corporate policy for Facebook posts and indeed for each platform you use.

- Ask fans/'likers' for feedback on your product/services via questions in posts, or links to surveys.

- Post good news on your business: sector-specific general updates; insightful, people-based anecdotes about your organization; only use humour that will work for your audience/culture.
- Share YouTube video clips and other visuals of general interest as well as about your business.
- Reply to comments. Thank people for positive comments and post promptly with your viewpoint, to counter any negative comments.

Many of you will have passed on a positive message about a company to others and, in a sense, become an unpaid advocate of their brand. Take a look at the language they used that engaged your interest.

It's a fascinating exercise that can help your writing.

LinkedIn

LinkedIn is a professional B2B networking site for matters strictly related to business and careers. Blatant selling of products or services is disallowed. But employers do trawl for new talent on it, so write a great profile, showcasing your attributes (whether as a provider or seeker), so it can double up as a résumé/CV. You can even add a badge showing you are open to new work. Avoid words that are clichés that LinkedIn guidelines can help you identify. An example is 'dynamic problem-solver' – words that actually lose impact if everyone is using them.

Activity

Use LinkedIn to help you project 'brand you' (your personal brand) and make yourself discoverable. Start with a headline that sums up who you are and what you want.

Here are some fictitious examples:

1 Bart Wierks: Improving IT Systems – Seeking Career Opportunity

2 Carl Chapman: Change Management Guru 'Hire me and results guaranteed'

3 Monica Heiss: Senior Associate at XYZ Global Staffing Associates – 4,000 connections

Example 1: we see at a glance what Bart does and what he's seeking.

Example 2: Carl uses rather more expressive language. His words express his personal brand and self-belief but some people will cringe at the over-used and often inappropriate use of the word 'guru'.

Example 3: Monica feels that her position and her networking credentials speak for themselves.

Which style, if any, do you think works best? How would you write?

Instagram

Although Instagram appears primarily to be a visual site, if you look at their website you'll see how they confirm my writing advice. In their words: 'an engaging caption can inspire your followers to interact with your photos and videos or to purchase your products or services.'

They give the following five tips (and amplify each in a few sentences, worth checking out):

1 tell a story
2 ask questions

3 keep it short and sweet

4 maintain a consistent tone

5 encourage your followers to take action

TikTok

TikTok is a short-form video-making and -hosting service that has become a major platform in a very short time. In their words, their mission is 'to capture and present the world's creativity, knowledge and precious life moments.' This naturally covers a wide gamut of material, including business topics.

See the 'Get Started on TikTok' section on their website and you'll find a selection of videos on 'How to Write Captions'. These show you how to use the right hashtags, keywords and design to make your business-oriented posts more visible in the first instance and more discoverable longer term.

The various platforms actively want you to use them

Do take advantage of their specific tips on what works best at any given time. The really great news is that the tips are all along the lines I'm advocating throughout, set out in the four-step writing system in Chapter 2. The underlying principles of effective writing stand firm across time, for all writing tasks.

Social media platforms allow a refreshing element of creativity, for example in terms of font and layout options (and colour blocking, if the functionality is available), to help your messages stand out. But don't lose sight of the fact that your messages are still part of your corporate communication.

Newsletters, blogs, vlogs or microblog posts

Newsletters and blogs read like articles and inform. While printed newsletters and other materials have to explain background within the articles themselves, online newsletters, blogs, vlogs (video logs) or microblogs (such as Twitter posts) can easily refer to detailed information elsewhere online. Post regularly to keep material fresh and build up a readership that you hope will be loyal advocates.

Keep your paragraphs shorter than in print (some recommend four sentences maximum). As reading on a computer screen can be tiring, and reading on mobile devices can be 'on the go', you need to 'grab eyeballs' so people do read. Invite questions and comments (and add reply buttons) – as long as you plan to respond to these. Get involved with others' blogs too. Be discoverable and maintain visibility.

Podcasts

You might be surprised that I'm mentioning the very fast-growing communication medium of podcasts here, because they naturally major on audio, with or without visuals.

But once you start researching how to make a podcast, you soon find that the professionals advise you to have some sort of script, at least as a roadmap to help you plan its structure and keep to it once on air. It's up to you how much writing will help you navigate the podcast but here are some key points to assist your script:

- have a good title
- have an intro that engages interest, and maybe include a teaser to something of audience interest later in the podcast
- outline your structure and edit your key points
- keep the style conversational even in your notes – you don't want your podcast to sound like a report
- bring 'brand you' to the script
- stay mindful of the 'what's in it for them?' aspect of your podcast throughout
- have what's known as a good 'outro' that will lead to your desired *call to action* (more on this shortly) e.g. 'subscribe now', 'catch our next podcast'

How to avoid writer's block

Everyone can suffer from writer's block on occasion, especially if today's storytelling or personal narrative (as just two examples) weren't previously your thing! Some of the best advice I've seen is from entrepreneur Sir Richard Branson, founder of the Virgin Group. Some years back he wrote on LinkedIn:

> What do you talk to your friends about? What was that interesting article you read the other day? What was everyone chatting about in the office at lunch? Could there be a blog in that? More than likely, yes.

I personally find the big ideas often come when I'm away from my desk. Do you? When you're jogging perhaps, or cooking, or simply relaxing if you can, in your own space? This can be more easily achievable in a hybrid workplace. The 'in the office' Sir Richard talks about, can now be 'over that Zoom call' too. It's best not to crowd ourselves with detail if we're to be creative. And focusing on our littered email in-tray can certainly defeat that objective.

What excites people so much they want to share it?

You already have an idea about this and indeed, analysing across all channels, these messages get shared most:

- Lists and tips:
  - Especially things on how to work better, for example, 'How successful people stay calm', 'The three qualities of people I most enjoy working with', 'Ten top tips for leadership'.

- Articles that bring out an emotional response:
  - Positive emotions get a faster response on most channels, e.g. greatest, happiest, cutest, wow this is GREAT!

- o That doesn't mean that negative emotions don't work. 'Four destructive myths to banish' definitely gets shared. 'Do you know how many things you could be sued for?' will most likely work better for an insurer than 'We introduce our exciting new insurance product!' But choose your negatives carefully in a business context.

- Quotes:
  - o As with articles, people share emotions just as much (maybe more) than they share facts. Share others' words of wisdom or witticisms etc, and you can become part of the chatter. If the quotes are your own, you may have more influence – and lead the conversation.

- Verbs:
  - o Whether knowledge- or action-based; for example, know, prove, think, grab one now, hurry, don't miss out.

- Captivating captions/slogans that underpin and enhance a relevant and brilliant visual/picture/video, for example:
  - o Apple: 'Think different'
  - o Nike: 'Just do it'
  - o KitKat: 'Have a break... have a KitKat'

(Just listen to the sound of the 'k' in the KitKat slogan. You can almost hear the sound of the biscuit breaking! That's effective writing. Alliteration can also help engagement – for brands such as PayPal, Coca-Cola, Dunkin' Donuts as well as for articles or videos.)

- Posts with calls to action (more on this shortly)

- Facts and infographics

See how Step 3 in the Word Power Skills system in Chapter 2 – 'Make the right impact' – will help you greatly here.

Call people to action – and check it's worked

An important element of social media is checking that it worked. If you go unnoticed, it might as well be money down the drain. So it never harms to hammer home this message: build in effective calls to action as if your life depended on it! You want people to react. Better, you want them to discuss positively, even evangelize. Mostly in business we need buy-in and sales.

Express, where feasible, what you want people to do next, *in all your written tasks*. Your focus in social media may be selling messages about brand, but you can still hope to convert to sales at a later date. Invite readers to subscribe to your newsletter or contact you. You can ask people:

- to *share* some piece of content, citing the source (industry insights, other knowledge, observations, news, your own tips, etc)
- to *like* on various channels
- to *retweet* what you say (evangelism can achieve sales too)

The hard fact is that without sales and profits, your core business can flounder.

Tips for writing calls to action

- Explain why (one or more major benefits).
- Enable people to respond.
- Communicate clearly what customers will get.
- Offer a realistic deadline and the benefits for the customer of acting quickly (a free offer/discount/upgrade/limited edition/ pegged interest rates, etc).
- Highlight dates or events that can be useful to your demographic. The more national, multicultural or international you become or want to become, the more hooks you can use, e.g. Christmas, Sinterklaas, Thanksgiving, Diwali, Eid, etc.

- By showing you understand issues of relevance to the world out there (where your current and prospective clients reside) you can become the trusted friend they will turn to for advice. Once they see that your advice comes from a place of values and knowledge, they're more likely to pay for targeted advice from 'that trusted friend' – or at least be an advocate for you to others.

Don't 'overthink' when you write. Don't lose sight of the essence of your business that you need to express throughout.

Your social media posts need to cross-refer to your website

Your website needs to act as a hub for your social media posts. All content should cross-refer and have a consistent look, feel and corporate style as part of the reader experience. So, just as with your social media posts, do your messages stand out with the 'power words' that reflect your values? Was your website originally written in a traditional style? Just as it had to be adapted for mobile devices, might it have to be further adapted to align with how you write for social media?

Now people expect bite-sized messages, headlined and subheadlined to break up text for scan reading. Make everything discoverable.

Finally, if your website is in English, do you use this in a global or local context? With the potential to reach out to new territories via social media too, writing effectively in English means one size won't fit all.

Telling your story

We've looked at many examples of how companies project their voice and personality in social media and how they tell their brand story, drawing readers into it and being interested in readers' stories too.

By now you should have a definite idea of what story you have to tell, alongside your company's personality. It's your exciting challenge to write vibrant content that draws people towards you.

So what's *your* compelling story? What did it begin with? Where are you at? Where are you going? Are you going to let readers share your people's stories and see their personalities? And are you going to invite your audience to share their stories?

There are no rights and wrongs here. As a checklist we could add:

- Never lose sight of your objectives and your readers' needs and expectations.

- How will you adapt your tone for the demographic (sector, culture, generation) you target?

- How will you get them to respond?

- How will you maintain interaction, as positively as possible?

- Are you asking the right questions? Are you getting the answers you hope for?

- Who will be there to respond to their questions – or their complaints, if any? (In social media, people expect rapid response.)

- How could your communication better lead to building the community you desire?

This chapter has shown you how companies write for these social media platforms for different reasons. They are largely to do with a desire to get individuals to help them get their name out there, even go viral, to develop and maintain a good global reputation. Just as a company needs to be responsive to customers when writing for social media, it needs to respond by revising corporate writing generally, as times move on. Just as business writing expressions such as 'hereunder', 'the aforesaid', 'we remain your obedient servants' and so on have been ditched over the past few decades, companies need to identify what becomes currently mainstream. Language evolves so policies need to as well, otherwise, once again, widely differing corporate styles can confuse readers and work against brand.

Everything has to be consummately professional because reputation matters – and it's easy for inferior writing to go viral for all the wrong reasons!

Be consistent in your storytelling in all your communication

And having identified your storytelling for social media, don't forget to be consistent in your storytelling style on your website too. We looked at financial institution Nationwide's stated values in Chapter 3, so now let's look at how they maintain consistency and follow through in their storytelling.

CASE STUDY   Nationwide member stories

Nationwide write up 'Member stories' on their website. In one case they feature how they are helping a student named Ibi 'achieve her dreams' and how their banking app is helping her do just that. They write: 'As we grow, it's natural that our priorities change. The things we save for and spend our money on change too.'

They develop a storyline that is easy to navigate via subheadings on the following lines:

She loves our banking app
From checking savings goals and account balances to shifting money between accounts, Ibi uses the app all the time. 'It makes it so easy to transfer money or see how much money I've got in my accounts.'

The Savings Goal feature is helping Ibi get to Japan
With her love of Japanese food, and anime, Japan fascinates Ibi. So it won't come as a surprise that she wants to visit the country. The

banking app helps Ibi save the money she needs. 'The Savings Goal feature tells me how much I need to save each day, week or month for my holiday.'

The app has saved Ibi a lot of stress
Like many of us, she's no stranger to misplacing her debit card now and again. Being able to freeze it with the app has been a bit of a life saver. 'It's usually in a coat pocket! So I just unfreeze it when I find it.'

There's ease and convenience too
The app means she can put her ideas into action the moment she has them. 'I was sat in my bedroom and thought I need to start saving some serious money to buy a house.' Ibi opened her Help to Buy ISA right there and then.

What do you think of this approach? My analysis is on these lines:

1 This type of storytelling is a development that we see across the board. It's a far more condensed version of the storytelling of some years back.

2 The storylines are very short and broken down into bite-sized, accessible snippets.

3 Each highlights a positive feature that the company wants people to see as a benefit of joining.

4 Ibi is portrayed sympathetically: we understand what makes her tick and what her concerns are.

5 We hear her actual words which adds authenticity to the story.

6 The story is firmly aligned to aspects that fit the company's purpose.

7 The story is not fully about Ibi – it's as much about Nationwide, enticing buy-in from people generally.

Activity

This chapter has given you plenty of advice on how to write for social media. Don't let it stop there! Take the opportunity of crafting a post for one of the channels here:

....

....

....

....

....

Even better, ask colleagues to do the same, and trade ideas. Being creative gets easier with practice and can be fun!

For most organizations this is the tricky part when it comes to storytelling and effective business writing. What's the balance between the story about the person or people you write about and your business purpose?

Your checklist for action

- How do you plan to write for social media? What are your objectives? Which channels will you use?
- How are you going to communicate 'brand you' (described in Chapter 3), as well as your values?
- Design writing that is discoverable by and relevant to your target audience.
- Be social when you write! Get involved. Maintain interaction, so you create a following/community and benefit from loyal brand advocates.

- Don't see social media writing as an inferior form of business communication; be professional and mind your and others' reputation. Mistakes can rapidly go viral!

- Check that everyone in your company, as well as in any outside agency you hire, understands how to project your voice: sometimes personal, always corporate.

- Keep up with emerging channels; tailor your writing and formatting for readers' business and cultural expectations.

- Analyse the language used in posts that work (these can be others' posts, not just your own); adapt your vocabulary and embrace the fact that language evolves.

- Ensure that your message is consistent across all your communication channels.

- Connect your story to your readers' stories and needs.

- Use the Word Power Skills writing system as it will continue to work across emerging channels too.

- Enjoy this opportunity to be creative!

06
Standard or variant English – and changing punctuation and grammar

If our written words 'clothe our logic', we need to choose the 'right clothes' and 'the right accessories' for the occasion!

The English language vs business English

English is a major language of commercial communication and a world language of the internet and of global access to knowledge, spoken by around a quarter of the world's population. As mentioned at the outset, this book isn't about teaching you the English language. It does assume a knowledge of English to intermediate level or above but if you want to develop your English language skills further, do seek out the excellent learning resources that are out there.

The *business English* element, which this book is about, is a specialized language which continues to evolve, just as its 'parent language' does. So it's strange how a lot of businesses don't actually define *what they mean* by business English. It can be a must if you work in a multicultural team, a cosmopolitan office, a multinational organization, or have a potential global reach through social media.

You may still have to design communication that specifically covers the many variants you'll encounter. So here are some common workplace scenarios you'll encounter.

'Standard' and 'variant' English

Did you know that globally, there are actually more *non-native speakers of English* than native English speakers? It belongs to no single culture but acts as a bridge across borders and cultures.

When I first worked abroad, I saw how multinationals wanted to seize the competitive edge in their use of English as a global business language. I realized how puzzled both foreigners and native English speakers can be by the way English is so often used. Sometimes it's because non-native English speakers use it in unconventional ways. Sometimes it's because people don't realize that UK English differs from the many other variations of business English that exist. These include US or American English, Australian English, Caribbean English, Indian English, Singapore English and South African English. It's an extensive list. Business communication is crucial to success. So if people are puzzled by it, this is bad news. Getting the right messages out and receiving the right answers are the lifeblood of commercial success. I found it helped my clients communicate effectively cross-culturally by following some norms of 'standard' English. The result? People understood each other!

So what is 'standard' English? I use it to mean the English routinely described in mainstream English dictionaries and grammar books. It's the English used throughout this book, likely to be understood by all users.

Unless I indicate otherwise, you're probably noticing the spelling and grammar used are the UK English variety requested by my publishers, to follow their house style. One of the challenges in writing UK English is that there can be more than one correct way of spelling certain words, as I've mentioned earlier. For example: 'recognize' and 'recognise', 'judgment' and 'judgement', 'e-mail' and 'email' can all be used correctly in UK English.

At times I refer to US English as well, where there are clearly divergent spellings or meanings. But the book won't address differences between UK and US English in detail. The important thing is: know that you need to check. This takes me to my next point.

Understand the business English conventions your audience follows

Whenever we write, we must understand the conventions to follow, if we're to please our target readers. If necessary, explain at the outset which you use so you can avoid unfounded or unnecessary criticism. One thing's sure: if someone can find grounds for criticizing writing, they will! Be one step ahead and, if asked, understand which variant you're using and why.

Be consistent, to underpin a strong, quality-conscious corporate image. You undermine this if some people in your company use UK English spellcheck and grammar check and others use US English versions in their communication. I see this done all the time. Do you? It's usually because no one has bothered to issue professional corporate guidelines.

Writing for both native and non-native English speakers

You'll have noticed that when I refer to native English speakers this means anyone who speaks any variety of English as their first language.

If you're a non-native English speaker, you may know these categories: English as an acquired language (EAL), English as a foreign language (EFL), English for speakers of other languages (ESOL) and English as a second language (ESL). If you're a native English speaker, have the courtesy to understand how others may have extra challenges when faced with your writing. Put it another way: could you easily understand business writing in a foreign language? Do keep that in mind. Communicators so often need more empathy, on every level.

As this book is designed to be suitable for all, it's useful to understand the terms I use are:

- a *native English (NE) speaker or writer* means someone whose first language is English, and native English (NE) writing to refer to their writing

- a *non-native English (non-NE) speaker or writer* means someone whose first language is not English, and non-native English (non-NE) writing to refer to their writing

Some surprising problems with English for global business

As well as there being different varieties of English, there are, in effect, sub-varieties directly caused by mixing English with the language patterns of the native country. Examples are Chinglish (Chinese English), Manglish (Malaysian English) and Singlish (Singaporean English).

Sometimes this can lead to out-and-out mistranslations. Although users may understand what they mean, these can be unintentionally funny or unintelligible to the foreign reader, as the following real-life mistranslated signs show. I deliberately don't highlight the countries concerned as it would be unfair to single any out. These mistakes occur across the board:

- sign over an information booth: 'Question Authority'
- sign in a maternity ward: 'No children allowed'

- sign in a restaurant: 'Customers who find our waitresses rude ought to see our manager'
- in an airline ticket office: 'We take your bags and send them in all directions'
- in a hotel lift/elevator: 'Please leave your values at the front desk'

The point is: do address the problem (even get professional help if needed), and check that your messages say what you intend them to say, especially in a global context, to people at differing levels of proficiency in English.

Let's now look at a sample of anglicized words used in Western Europe. Expressions such as 'a parking' (UK English: a car park; US English: a parking lot) or 'presentation charts' (UK and US English: presentation slides) are used predominantly in Germany, as well as words such as 'handy' in continental Europe (UK English: mobile phone; US English: cell phone), or 'beamer' in France and elsewhere (UK English: projector). But if we are writing globally, by definition, we're not just writing for readers in one country.

If the vast majority of English speakers have no idea what these sorts of 'pseudo-anglicisms' mean, this can lead to unintended problems.

So do define business English within your company

Ensure the terms you use really are understood by your target audience. Terms understood in Western Europe may not have the same currency in Asian markets and so on. Certain English-sounding words may have crept into your usage but it doesn't mean they are internationally recognized.

Activity

Gain consensus via colleagues and readers on the business English you plan to use at any given time.

Get in the habit of using words that are easily accessible.

Flag up words that you identify will not be easily understood – or may actually have different meanings in a different variant of English. You can jot them down here.

....

....

....

....

....

Standard or variant punctuation? It's all about context

Does this question surprise you? I could in fact ask 'do we need to punctuate or not?' because I'm going to show how the world is changing in this respect.

It's fascinating to research the history of punctuation in English, and *The English Project's History of English Punctuation* by Christopher Mulvey provides a concise insight. In the past, punctuation has undergone many transformations, and it will continue to do so. There have been very noticeable shifts just this century.

The reason that widely accepted standards emerged in the first place was for clarity and consistency. Some sort of organized punctuation helped publishers standardize printing presses, as that's how written information began to be widely disseminated. Now we see new punctuation possibilities emerge, as more casual writers on the web don't necessarily adhere to the rigorous standards of the past. This doesn't mean that anarchy should prevail: messages still need to be understood easily to work best. As Mulvey explains:

> Punctuation is a communal thing. A use has to be agreed by a group, but it does not have to be agreed by everyone. You'll want your group to be as large as possible, perhaps, but, if you establish a conventional use and others follow you, then you have a functional punctuation mark.

This is helpful in understanding what's going on in today's workplace.

Standard punctuation

This extract shows what unpunctuated writing looks like:

> mr jones the companys hr director called mrs smith into his office for an update on the latest recruitment drive he wanted to know whether the online application system was working reports had filtered through that all was not going to plan mrs smith explained that candidates were certainly experiencing problems as the systems had crashed in her opinion it would be better to extend the closing date would he be prepared to authorize this

Did you have any problem deciphering this? A lot of people will find it difficult. If we write poetry we may actively want people to work out the meaning. We may even want them to create their own meaning; but this should not apply to business writing!

Standard punctuation taught in schools in the past and in traditional English language learning, generally, was intended as an aid to help readers understand our traditionally written messages. Even using these standards, the extract could be punctuated a number of ways. I will use one way to show how it becomes easier to read:

> Mr Jones, the company's HR director, called Mrs Smith into his office for an update on the latest recruitment drive. He wanted to know whether the online application system was working. Reports had filtered through that all was not going to plan.

Mrs Smith explained that candidates were certainly experiencing problems as the systems had crashed. In her opinion, it would be better to extend the closing date.

Would he be prepared to authorize this?

Unless you're exclusively writing casual text messages or social media posts, you'll find that traditional punctuation is still very much alive in today's workplace. If like many people you find some aspects challenging, do ask a line manager or a mentor if you need help. Ideally, managers should be encouraged to offer active support to people with dyslexia or other neurodiverse writing challenges.

Top entrepreneur Richard Branson is dyslexic yet has written best-selling business books and much-admired blogs. He says he relies on his right-hand people to check his English before he publishes because he knows that this does matter. That's inspirational.

The best leaders encourage supportive teamwork, so companies get things right on all levels.

Variant punctuation in texting and social media

Mostly everyone in today's workplace is a writer in their social life too, thanks to writing being the principal driver of internet communication. But there aren't necessarily the overseers such as editors, or even censors, to revise messages sent out. As writing is the new talk, people tend to use a more spontaneous, stream-of-consciousness style – writing thoughts as they occur to them. I think this can be a reason managers are often complaining that increasingly, staff aren't getting to the point when they write. Long-winded writing, also known as *waffle* or *gobbledygook*, is rearing its ineffective head!

But let's just analyse here the phenomenon of what I call variant punctuation in texting and social media posts in corporate communication.

I'll address writing email and instant messaging in more detail in Chapter 8 but need to introduce the phenomenon of 'variant punctuation' in this section, as we also see it in social media. Punctuation marks today can signify more than grammar features: they can signify emotions too. For instance, now that hitting *enter* shows when our instant message or social media post ends, the period or full stop can be viewed as redundant. Many think that inserting it signifies 'the conversation' is over and the 'discussion ended'.

For this reason, full stops/periods can increasingly be considered passive–aggressive, even though this may be completely unintended by the writer.

Be aware of this as this interpretation is also spilling over into social media and website posts where open punctuation is also more prevalent.

There are many more interesting observations too, as the study 'Punctuation in text messages helps replace cues found in face-to-face conversations' by Celia Klin, Professor of Psychology at Binghamton University in New York, shows (Klin, 2017).

Her study suggests that:

Emoticons, irregular spellings and exclamation points in text messages aren't sloppy or a sign that written language is going down the tubes — these… help convey meaning and intent in the absence of spoken conversation.

The study also suggests, among other things, that:

One way that texters add meaning to their words is by using 'textisms'— things like emoticons, irregular spellings (sooooo) and irregular use of punctuation (!!!).

Do check the report out for more insights.

Activity

In the light of this, imagine a manager has sent a message to a WhatsApp group: 'Are you ok with this suggestion?'

And the answers come back:

yes

Yes.

yessss
YES
Yes!

How might you interpret each of these answers, in the light of the punctuation that 'accessorizes' the word – and which can tell us a lot about how the reader felt?

I would suggest that:

- The first replier (*yes*) was ok with the suggestion.

- The second one (Yes.) might have been using traditional punctuation and was ok with the suggestion. Conversely, the newer use of this punctuation might be registering that they weren't fully on board!

- The third replier (yessss – which we see increasingly in social media posts) appears enthusiastically in agreement (and this can show others' agreement to be flatter in contrast!)

- The fourth replier (YES) is using punctuation that can indicate shouting and could therefore be in disagreement, despite the affirmative word used. On the other hand, the capitals can be interpreted as expressing support!

- The fifth replier is using an exclamation mark which is increasingly used to convey enthusiasm in texting (as in other writing).

Ellipsis

An ellipsis, usually appearing as three dots in a sentence or phrase (...), is another punctuation mark now used creatively in business writing today. Originally, an ellipsis indicated that something had been left out of the writing intentionally, that did not affect the overall meaning, e.g. 'The government doesn't intend to change the law... it's for the next administration to do this.' The writer didn't feel it necessary to explain (presumably again) which law they were referring to. Alternatively, an ellipsis could suggest a pause, e.g. 'That's a great idea... we'll implement it next week.'

But what we can now sometimes see is an ellipsis used to signify:

- conversational 'hmms' or 'erms' to soften the text
- indicators of 'food for thought' for writer and/or reader alike (e.g. 'let's see... might work) which don't necessarily lead to action
- less positive meanings such as impatience or dissent (e.g. This will work?... where the ellipsis implies: 'No it won't!')

Asterisks

The traditional use of an asterisk (*) was to indicate a footnote below the text where further clarifying information can be found. Now we also see asterisks used for emphasis, usually in texting or social media, where font types are unavailable, e.g.:

'I *really* want to see that'

Tune in to the changes and check understanding

As changes in punctuation and readers' reactions will continue to evolve, we all need to tune in and routinely check that not just our words, but our punctuation too, are saying what we mean them to say, and as positively as possible. In the absence of traditional editing, it's up to each of us to keep on top of this.

In similar cases that you may encounter, if you are in any doubt at all check with a colleague. It's important that all are 'literally on the same page' and it can prevent unnecessary complications, including hurt feelings which are a massive contributor to the sense of a toxic workplace. I do feel that ineffective writing is a massively under-researched factor in this respect.

Make a difference by injecting positivity and enthusiasm where you can and removing misunderstandings when you write. We all know that positivity can be contagious as can negativity. And you know which you prefer, and which your readers generally are likely to prefer, don't you?

Context matters

So yes, you're going to come across a real mix between standard and variant punctuation and we all need to accept that language changes according to context. But it'll never make commercial sense to revert to the completely unpunctuated form of writing in the earlier exercise. No business can afford to produce ineffective writing that is virtually indecipherable.

Grammar can change too

This book isn't a grammar guide. But I do need to alert you to the fact that you'll also see changing grammar patterns emerging at times. The term 'grammar' serves to describe the features of a language and how we organize those features – for example, into sentences and paragraphs, so that those we communicate with will understand us clearly. That's the important consideration and the yardstick you need to use.

What I would like to do now is look at some areas you will encounter frequently in a business context.

Personal pronouns

In English grammar, words are categorized into what we term parts of speech. These include nouns, pronouns, adjectives, verbs, adverbs, prepositions, conjunctions and interjections.

A noun names a person, place or thing. For example:

girl, London, newspaper

A pronoun is a word that can take the place of a noun which is basically the name of a person, place or thing. A pronoun functions like a noun. For example:

I, this, who, he, they

There's Gamal who won the lottery.

Notice how the noun 'Gamal' became the pronoun 'who' within the same sentence.

Tune in to the changing use of pronouns in business today. My publishers offer guidelines as follows. Avoid using masculine pronouns for neutral nouns. Use 'they' and 'their' rather than 'he', 'him', 'his'.

In this way, you will find an example such as this: 'Not sure what to do? Ask your manager for their advice.' Even though 'manager' is a singular noun, the neutral plural 'their' is common usage now, in this context.

Moreover, more pronouns are being added to the mix of English pronouns found in traditional grammar books of yesteryear. Not everyone identifies as 'he' or 'she'. Some people prefer 'they'/'them' pronouns, beyond binary gender. Others may indicate personal, gender-fluid pronouns they want you to use when addressing them, such as 'ze' or 'hir' as their preferred third-person singular pronouns over 'he' or 'she' etc.

There are many other variations that this book hasn't the scope to include, and besides, it is very much about individuals' personal preferences, so please do take the time to research your readers, ask them if possible, and have the respect to mirror to them what they expect.

Also, many companies are encouraging employees to indicate their personal pronouns in their email signatures and social media bios, as a tangible pointer of inclusivity.

So do tailor your writing by tuning in to all ongoing changes. Communicate effectively and respectfully with your target audience.

Paragraphs and other aids to structure

Another way to 'accessorize' your words is by designing helpful paragraphs. Paragraphs help readers understand the organization of your writing because each paragraph is a group of sentences about a topic. Key messages become easy to identify and the format makes it easy for you to develop them. Paragraph headings (and subheadings so often used on the web) are increasingly used to signpost messages and highlight structure for readers' ease.

Brackets, bullet points and dashes

These are all aids you've seen me use throughout the book to break up text so readers are not overwhelmed with information, and you can also use commas, as I am doing here, to make a longish sentence more manageable.

Bullet points are used more and more frequently, not just for readability, and have the added bonus of helping you structure your points.

On the reverse side, too many short sentences can seem abrupt. So keep your writing interesting by mixing and matching these features, to vary and enhance your style.

Helpful subheadings

You can see I have used subheadings throughout the book, to help you navigate your way through the subject matter, using key words that you would likely type into a search engine for the information you seek.

Once you start thinking in this way, you soon become more structured in your approach to every writing task. It becomes second nature – and readers (internally and externally) will thank you for it!

Questions

Writing is the new talking, as we're examining in detail in the book, so it's no surprise that we'll use conversational-style questions in our business writing. But how to write them? It may seem clear to native English speakers but non-NE speakers can find them quite tricky. So here are some tips.

Speakers and writers use question tags to encourage their listeners or readers to respond. It helps check that people agree or understand what you are saying or writing.

Examples of question tags

'It's a good outcome, isn't it?'

'You don't have a meeting today, do you? You can make it in time, can't you?'

Examples of incorrect usage

'You have got the right files, isn't it?'

'He is wrong, doesn't he?'

'These kind of things are dealt with in your department, isn't it?'

Correct versions

'You have got the right files, haven't you?'

'He is wrong, isn't he?'

'These kinds of things are dealt with in your department, aren't they?'

- Try balancing the same verb (including whether it is singular or plural) on either side of the sentence.
- Then use a negative in the end questioning part of the sentence.

Beware of unintended interpretations of questions!

Apart from the standard questioning I've just outlined, we increasingly see some other forms, such as a manager writing to colleagues:

'That was the plan, no?'

What the manager may or may not realize is that colleagues' unseen reactions may be:

- in agreement: 'Yes, that was the plan'
- to view this as a 'passive–aggressive question' by which I mean they read between the lines, thinking the manager is implying an overt, or unexpressed criticism
- to register that the manager is actually surprised that that was the plan and is simply checking that, with no criticism implied

Do you see what I mean? And which interpretation would you be likely to make?

So, I think it's a case where traditional question formats work better. They are less likely to be open to misinterpretation.

Open and closed questions

Also when you write English across cultures, do be aware that closed questions typically lead to a yes/no/factual answer. Examples are:

'Please can you complete this report by month end?'

'Is the presentation ready?'

If you are dealing with a reserved culture, it could be a better idea to use an open question, such as:

'Please could you give an indication of when you can complete this?'

'What do you think?'

The recipient then has to give a fuller and more informative answer. By writing the right thing at the outset, you get the result you need.

Activity

Do you or your colleagues find any aspects of traditional or changing punctuation and grammar a challenge? It's well worth jotting down any points you feel you need to look at individually, or as teams.

....

....

....

....

....

Your checklist for action

- Understand that business English is a variety of the English language, with different subsets.

- Do you communicate with a specific group of business English users? Or are you likely to be communicating worldwide?

- Do you need to vary your business English subset according to your target audience each time?

- Do you set your computer spellcheck and grammar check to the type(s) of English you use?

- If so, do you check that it doesn't default to, say, US English spelling (unless that's your preferred variety)?

- Are you keeping up to speed with the differences in business English between 'standard' punctuation and grammar and emerging 'variants'?

- Are you using the appropriate style for your readership?

- Are you regularly checking that readers are getting the same meaning from the punctuation and grammar used?
- Do you also regularly check that the words you use are understood by your readers?
- When you don't understand a word, be confident and ask its meaning – this is a sign of strength, not weakness.
- Regularly feed back your findings to colleagues and encourage their buy-in.

Reference

Klin, C (2017) Punctuation in text messages helps replace cues found in face-to-face, Binghamton University, www.binghamton.edu/news/story/873/study-punctuation-in-text-messages-helps-replace-cues-found-in-face-to-face (archived at https://perma.cc/42VN-CGQ6)

07
Writing globally? Or in multinational teams?

Get everything in focus – and check that your words have international and cultural currency. Clarity matters for all!

Looking at how you use English at work

The mirror features largely in how we post in a social media age. We care about the optics. People want to present the best photographic image of themselves in highly visual channels such as Instagram and TikTok.

So let's develop this theme where our writing is concerned, as well. Why stop short of presenting the best image you can, here too?

Where's your focus when many cultures are involved?

So hold up a figurative mirror to try to evaluate:

- how your readers see themselves
- how you see yourself – and your organization

- how you see your readers
- how your readers may see you through your writing

As the images will tend to diverge, you write successfully when you remove distortions, bringing the four equally important images together into sharp, correct focus.

Different cultures can communicate differently

If you're dealing with a particular country, research how to communicate with their culture. Don't overlook the fact that multicultural teams may also be found in your home workplace.

In outline, it's true to say that a typical Western style of writing comes over as structured and fairly direct (that said, you may still encounter waffle: lots of words with no clear purpose!).

If we look at Asian cultures, we can find extremely polite, formal, self-effacing communication. It can be considered bad style to get to the point too quickly and rude to make points too directly. Such cultures are likely to have a stronger focus on introduction, setting a respectful tone, developing rapport, only then ending on the main points (which they may imply rather than express).

Do address the cultural and the many other aspects of diversity in the workplace that determine the writing style needed for each task. We saw in Chapter 5 how companies can tailor their marketing to the culture and terminology expected in their target audience. Keep this in mind when you communicate in everyday life with international readers too. Let's look at some examples to illustrate.

Writing for cultures accustomed to saying 'yes'

It really helps to understand that some cultures will say 'yes' in their business writing because their culture might frown on saying 'no'. This can be because:

- they may feel they will come over as unprofessional – even 'lose face'

- they may believe they will be seen as uneducated – even foolish if they have not understood
- they may feel that people will think they lack resilience (particularly important in Asian cultures)
- they may prefer to be conciliatory and avoid disagreement

Where you know these reactions may be likely, adapt your writing. I've touched in Chapter 6 how open questions can really help. I can add here another tool: *summarize questions at the end of relevant messages*, to check, respectfully and accurately, that all the different cultures have understood points made. For example, a manager could write:

> So can we confirm, do we all agree that we delay completion of this project for a month? If anyone doesn't agree I'd value your input. Let me know why (in the next couple of days please), and we can have a rethink, as to what we do next.

Yes, there are quite a lot of words. But if words add value and aid performance on many levels, you see how these contribute to effective writing.

Writing for cultures accustomed to saying 'no'

Conversely, some cultures have no problem at all saying 'no'. They see it as supremely efficient – and certainly it's less wordy. But efficiency isn't always about word count, as we've just seen. What 'no' cultures don't see is the potentially offended faces of readers from the 'yes' or 'maybe' cultures. They may not see the one word 'no' as efficient but rude. For example:

Question: Please can you let me have the answer tomorrow?

Answer: No.

The questioner just needs to appreciate that readers from different cultures may absolutely need to see context and reasons explained. On this basis, the message could be easily adapted to work effectively:

Question: I'm afraid I can't get the information to you tomorrow, as it's still being prepared. Will the day after tomorrow be alright with you?

This brings the level of mutual understanding and inclusivity that's needed to make everyone in the target readership feel valued. It also helps teams pull together.

Also, the writer hasn't had to shift their position. What they have done is understand, as this book is showing throughout, that effective business writing gives people *the right feeling* alongside producing *the right performance*.

New jobs, mergers and acquisitions… scenarios that can challenge

You might have chosen a new job that now involves business English writing. Although it's your choice, you're likely to want to develop your confidence in this skill. But imagine if the requirement to write in English is foisted upon a non-native English speaker through a merger or acquisition. That can be a real and possibly unwanted challenge for them.

The key to success has to be to ask for training if it applies to you. And if you manage multicultural teams, empathize and offer the support that's needed!

Do your words say what you think they say? This applies to all!

Have you ever had to explain to readers: 'Oh, I didn't mean that'? If so, you won't be alone – and this actually applies everywhere – for our home and international readership!

That's why major UK companies and government agencies, as well as smaller players, all call me in as a troubleshooter to check over their business writing for native readers too! Are their words (to internal and external customers, suppliers and in technical documents, etc) *really* saying what they want them to say? It's not just a plain English issue: it's also about adopting the right frame of mind to make the right connections with readers. Stand back – and see your writing from all angles. An undoubtedly well-intentioned writer in Australia didn't do this when advertising literacy classes, as the text of this poster shows:

Are you an adult that cannot read? If so, we can help you.

The poster was actually aimed at those who knew adults that cannot read, therefore, logically, it should have been worded differently. The moment you say 'I didn't mean that!' is the moment you realize that no, your writing isn't saying what you meant.

Activity

I'm sure that some written message you've seen at work recently didn't accurately say what was intended. It happens to us all, daily!

Did you write something, send it – and then wish you'd expressed it differently because people got back to you with the wrong reaction? Or maybe a colleague or supplier had to explain something they'd sent? Did the query (or even problem) arise because of a language or cultural misunderstanding? Or was it simply because your message could have been worded more clearly?

Take a minute to ask others too and why not jot your findings down here:

....

....

....

....

....

Empathize with the extra challenges for non-native English speakers

The last point brings me to this observation. We all face real challenges as to how we convert our thoughts into words – and convey meaning precisely. Writing words down can bring additional problems. Will the words work on paper or on the screen, when we're not there to explain them?

The factors that can distort intended meanings can naturally be a far greater challenge for non-native speakers of English. They may need to translate their words from their native language into English first, before writing. If this applies to you, a systematic approach can help:

1 Identify the thought effectively in your own language.

2 Translate it correctly from your own language into English.

3 You may then need to convert the thought captured in English into the correct *written* English word.

4 Then make sure that the 'correct written English word' is one your readers will understand.

5 Having done all this, your English writing should enable readers to respond the way you want. That's what you're in business for!

Let's see how we can all minimize any further distortions from planning stage through to delivery.

Straight translation may not work

We've looked at the need for plain, accessible English in earlier chapters, and now let's look at how important it is in the international arena. If you're a non-native English (non-NE) writer, don't just think you need to translate your own language into English because it can result in:

• over-complicated or incorrect messages

• focusing on the specific words rather than the overall meaning

- losing focus on the business need: for example, to write an essential call to action (what to do next)

Choosing unnecessarily complicated words rarely sits well in the modern workplace. For example, 'erudite' is a 'correct' word that crops up in translation but it's not a clever word if your readers don't understand it. Or use precious time in trying to. Similarly, why write verbose sentences such as 'the information we have assembled leads us to believe that...' over the more accessible 'we find that...'. The age of short attention spans adds weight to this observation.

Also, don't make assumptions when you translate a word such as *actualmente* from Spanish to English that it will be the similarly sounding English word 'actually'. The correct word would be 'currently'. Don't guess at meanings, or make your readers do the same.

Regularly ask yourself:

- Will my readers recognize the words I use?
- Will they understand their meaning easily?
- Will these words attract and continue to engage their attention?
- Am I easily enabling the response I need?

Look for the word that people really use. Don't be disappointed if this is more prosaic than the language of Shakespeare. You write intelligently in English for business when your readers understand you.

Collaboration across cultures involves asking if unsure, and sharing tips

Problems that can arise from non-NE writing affect non-NE and native English readers alike. You'll see scenarios like this:

- we can't understand some or any of the non-NE writer's writing
- we *almost* understand what is meant but don't ask questions as we should (either out of goodwill, or because of our cultural reservation – or because we can't be bothered!)

- the wrong meaning then continues to be communicated, which can lead to all sorts of problems

As an illustration, Indian English uses the expression 'trial room' which in UK or US English is 'changing room' or 'fitting room' or 'dressing room', where people try on clothes in a store before buying. In a multinational discussion forum on which expression to use, participants were really interested in this Indian English expression. Many had assumed it must mean 'courthouse', which it certainly didn't. So if you're uncertain of a meaning that might sound familiar in English but isn't what you would expect, don't be afraid to question this.

You see, you'll also find scenarios where even native US or UK English speakers can be puzzled by different usage of an apparently common word, such as 'gas'. For both, the word relates to a state of matter but in US English it also means 'gasoline' – a fuel that in UK English is called 'petrol'. It's an instance, as in the previous cases I've discussed, where you may find yourself 'divided by a common language'. That's why, when in doubt, it's professional to check so you communicate effectively.

Do you work in or deal with multicultural teams? Or write for an international readership? Discussing what works and what doesn't is the essence of collaboration – and will bring you all much closer together in designing effective communication.

Some features regularly perplex *all* readers

The following can perplex both native English and non-NE writers alike.

Idioms, clichés and nuances

Idioms are expressions that are peculiar to a language. Simply by translating the words, non-NE speakers may be unable to work out their meanings. It's true you can feel great mastering some idioms in a foreign language. You might feel 'over the moon' about it. Or am I pulling the wool over your eyes? Are you completely puzzled?

Let me explain:

- 'Over the moon' means delighted.
- 'To pull the wool over someone's eyes' means to deceive them or obscure something from them.

One director told me he'd used an idiom in a message – and soon wished he hadn't. It was on the lines of:

'Let's go with the lie of the land.'

By this he meant:

'Let's see how the situation develops and go with that.'

The non-NE recipient didn't understand – and focused on a literal meaning of 'lie' as an untruth. Imagine his shock. What was the director suggesting? Quite rightly, he phoned to ask.

In the light of the extra five minutes taken to explain, and the unintended shocked reaction of the recipient, the director's note to self was: avoid idioms in the future!

And don't forget, native English speakers can be puzzled by idioms too. They can quickly become obsolete.

Let's consider clichés now. The word 'cliché' has been imported from French into many languages, but, interestingly, it doesn't always mean the same thing in each. In German, for example, it means a stereotype, whereas in UK English it means a stale expression: something that's ineffective through overuse. A cliché often overlaps with corporate jargon or management speak and can undermine writing.

Here are some examples of clichés, with their meanings shown in brackets:

- 'in this day and age' (now)
- 'pick the low-hanging fruit' (go for the easy option)
- 'think outside the box' (think in an original or creative way)

In a business context, using a 'nuance', that is, a subtlety in meaning between, say, 'quite proud' and 'proud' can lead to problems. To a British speaker 'proud' usually has a stronger emphasis than 'quite proud'. If I tell someone I'm proud of their work, it's an absolute. They have done very well and I'm telling them that. The moment I say that I'm 'quite proud', the perception can be that I'm diluting my pride: I am less proud than I could be. The nuance then implies that the person could have done better. That would make a material difference in a written performance review, for example.

But I once heard an American boss tell a member of staff that he was 'quite proud' of his achievements. I could hear his intonation in the spoken words. This distinctly told me that he was using 'quite proud' to mean 'very proud'. But we can't hear intonation in writing (except when we SHOUT through capital letters or via emojis etc). So written nuances that mean different things to different people might not make commercial sense when you think about it.

Activity

Are there any words or expressions that have puzzled you or others that you can readily recall?

Why not jot them down here while the subject is fresh in your mind?

Consider discussing your findings with colleagues in the spirit of positive collaboration, to get things right in the future.

....

....

....

....

....

Jargon, buzzwords and acronyms

Jargon is the name usually given to words or expressions used by a particular profession or group. In the business world it overlaps with management speak and buzzwords.

It's arguable that you can justifiably use it if it's something that everyone in the user group understands. For example, you might see:

'We're communicating in a vuca world.'

If you're familiar with this 'management speak', you'll know 'vuca' is an acronym – a word that's an abbreviation that uses initials of a phrase – and here it's shorthand for 'volatility, uncertainty, complexity and ambiguity'. The writer who uses it assumes the readership understands. This may be correct – but if not, it's actually excluding those 'not in the know'. And of course, in the age of digital, our communication can be forwarded, even without our knowledge, to others in a wider group who may not understand without some explanation.

So very quickly, something that was meant to be helpful can become an unexpected barrier. Watch out for this – and use jargon advisedly.

While on this subject, we regularly see outpourings of resentment on online forums against buzzwords as the 'new jargon'. You know the sort of thing:

- this is on my radar
- deep dive
- new normal
- let's push the envelope
- leverage yourself to bring your A game to the table

I'd like to see your expressions as you read them. I'm not going to explain what they mean, because that's the point of what I'm saying! They'll mean slightly different things to different people – and if used in your culture, or office subculture and so on, do check what they're *supposed* to mean. They're unlikely to be universal currency – and indeed can soon become yesterday's cast-off.

How to write acronyms

Some acronyms, e.g. of official global organizations, are of course very useful shorthand. When you first write one, the convention is to write the compound word in full and put the acronym in brackets after it. For example, World Health Organization (WHO). Subsequently you can just use the acronym, as readers will understand the meaning.

You can't just assume that readers will understand without doing that. For example, WWF can stand for World Wildlife Fund and also World Wrestling Federation – quite a different focus! And it's often the case that readers won't ask the meaning, sometimes because they can't be bothered, sometimes for fear of appearing foolish not to know.

Activity

Have you come across jargon, including management speak, in business English?

1   If so, are there examples that others use that you don't understand or that annoy you that you can jot down here?

....

....

....

....

2   Do you ever use jargon, including management speak, yourself? Can you jot any down here – and maybe check with a focus group from your target audience that they really do understand it?

....

....

....

....

Non-native English writers can have an advantage!

Forward-thinking, successful companies often actively encourage and train non-NE employees to perfect the English writing skills they need. A positive learning culture such as this cares about quality and professionalism. It can even result in non-NE staff making more effort than native speakers in avoiding confusion and misunderstandings.

Native English writers: beware of complacency!

Native speakers of any language can assume they are proficient in their own language, so 'of course people understand what we say and write'. But it's not necessarily true. Increasingly we see companies assess writing ability when recruiting and/or promoting employees into jobs that need this skill (and, actually, which jobs don't?). Otherwise complacency sets in – and complacency drains the lifeblood of any organization. It's how companies lose the competitive edge.

It's certainly not just non-native English writers who make mistakes. But the uplifting fact is that, whatever the nationality, it's virtually always the talented who have the passion to strive to be better!

Your checklist for action

To use business English at work, your words and the framework that surround them have to be perfect. It's achievable; keep the bar high – don't set it lower! There are stark consequences of getting it wrong, as we keep seeing: business writing mistakes (including unclear, confusing or alienating messages) can equal lost cash, custom or goodwill.

For these reasons:

- Always present your best image, at the same time drawing all aspects of your business communication into the correct focus for the task in hand.

- Address and embrace diversity in your business writing too.

- Regularly check – both yourself and with readers, which naturally includes colleagues – that your words say what you mean them to say.

- Keep your focus on the cultures you're communicating with and adapt your writing.

- If you're a native English speaker, don't be complacent – empathize with the extra challenges non-native English speakers may face.

- Avoid features that can confuse, and use plain English where you can.

- Be inclusive, which can involve adding more words at times.

- Discuss any points arising from this chapter with colleagues.

- Flag up any general or specific concerns (especially helpful for bringing multicultural and/or multigenerational or other diverse teams closer).

- As always, collaboration matters – give it the attention it deserves.

08
Email and instant messaging

Instant works well for some messaging, email for others.

General

In email and instant messaging (IM), the focus is on the one-to-one recipient or the relatively 'captive audiences' of your thread or address book contacts.

Email interaction has the advantage of wide reach. It's asynchronous: it doesn't take place in real time. The reply you need might take hours, days, even weeks. It's fine if you're communicating over different time zones and you can't expect immediate replies. Or your message may need respondents to gather more information before they can answer effectively. In other instances, delays can be because recipients' in-trays are overflowing. We all know about that.

Instant messaging depends on your audience sharing the same networks. It can be synchronous if recipients are online at the same time. It works well when real-time conversation can enhance performance – for example where somebody needs to know the latest sales figures, or project updates, or when dealing with customer queries, complaints, etc.

In terms of style, it's interesting how email now seems 'traditional' writing – while IM is increasingly casual and emoji-laden.

One reason might be its obvious growth in an increasingly dispersed or hybrid workplace where employees work from home (WFH) on some days. Colleagues who previously might have chatted around the office water cooler yearn for the sociability that instant interaction afforded. And the casual conversational style of IM can fill a gap in this respect.

We see techs and young start-ups among the businesses preferring IM over email. Others, such as regulated financial or legal professions, use IM internally but not necessarily externally. Email can be their preferred medium as people tend to be more guarded in what they write. This can help to avoid the circulation of 'loose talk'.

Watch out for 'blurred lines' when mixing and matching channels

It's why each organization needs to think: to what degree can the casualness of social media IM in staff's 'out-of-hours' chat be carried over into workplace writing? In short, what's professional and what's not? It's a fact that all businesses, big and small, need to watch out for loose communication (that might even start as banter) that could lead to litigation in areas such as:

- equality
- harassment
- bullying
- trader knowledge
- personal data leaks etc

The chitchat around the water cooler wasn't recorded for posterity. But IM (and of course email) can be.

This book isn't about examining the technical pros and cons of each but I can describe the sort of writing that can work best.

Email

We know that inestimable billions of emails are sent worldwide each day. This doesn't mean to say volume equates with effectiveness as a business writing medium. Information overload is a massive problem. And it's no good having a big inbox with little content of relevance.

The best solution? Get to the point, but personably. Let readers see 'what do you want from me?' Give readers their time back and develop your logical skills at the same time. That's a huge career bonus.

It can mean checking each time you use email that it is the right medium. Would a phone call, face-to-face conversation or IM (more on this shortly) do the job more effectively?

Writing emails

Emails need structure to work efficiently. There's little training out there, so develop your skills and:

- write professionally, for your purpose, your organization's purpose and for your reader
- send to the right person/people at the right time
- be accurate and concise
- supply context as necessary (maybe as a link so that you don't ramble)
- have the right tone for the readership: not overly casual and not overly terse, even if (or especially if) the message is bearing harsh news
- where possible convey a virtual handshake to pull readers towards you and the company – not a push away

A good headline can help you and your readers

In a time of horribly littered in-trays, little wonder that stressed recipients often don't know where to begin when it comes to opening and then reading emails.

You'll know what I mean. So, if you can, design a headline that'll make readers more likely to want to open it.

Positivity can help

Contrast this notification to a team about better-than-expected trading figures in the last month:

'Trading figures last month'

with:

'Congratulations team! Great results!'

Intrigue can help

One time I wasn't getting a decision back from a company in the time frame I needed following a question I put to them. Creativity was needed to get their attention: Step 3 on the ladder of success writing system in Chapter 2. So I used this headline:

'Yes? No? Or maybe?'

And I received a reply (a yes, I was pleased to note) by return!

Microsoft Outlook caught my attention when they announced a change to the location of their shortcut button feature 'Coming Soon'. The headline to the change was presented as:

'Coming Soon will be going away shortly'

The play on words is simple yet intriguing, clearly designed to grab attention. I wanted to find out more. Would you? It's a technique to consider for creating interest and follow-up.

Phrase negativity with care

Of course, we all will have negative things to express in business. As you'll know, it can often be so much better to pick up the phone or say things face-to-face, softening the blow. If writing is a must, this sort of headline about a missed deadline or losing out on a bid, for example, introduces negativity in an empathetic way:

'We just missed out'

The writer of this headline might have thought they were softening the blow by introducing emotion:

'We've missed this deadline 😊'

But readers are likely to find this odd and confusing. Is missing a deadline something to celebrate? Have a think about what you might write in such a situation.

Avoid headings that are wrong

Name them correctly. Sometimes headings are wrong because they haven't been refreshed. You'll know the sort of thing – they confuse readers and undermine audit trails and even results. For example, look at this heading:

'Quarter 3 update'

Understandably, you would expect the message will be about Quarter 3. But if when you open it, the sender has attached the figures for Quarter 4 then it's not just ineffective, it doesn't reflect well on the sender's organizational skills.

Even salutations and sign-offs can make all the difference

You'll remember that at the outset of the book I suggested we can actually make a difference for the better, even just a few words at a time. You've been seeing this throughout, and here's another easy way. You see you can actually impress readers (or annoy them!) right from how you start and end emails.

You won't see your readers' faces, but they'll have expressions when they react to your words. Naturally you can't always elicit smiles, but you can aim for goodwill. And definitely try not to foster frowns.

Take a look at some common examples in the box.

Example 1

Email starter: Hi Jaxon

Annoyed reply: My name is Jackson

Getting someone's personal details wrong is a universal irritant and can be taken as rude. It's always best to check if you're unsure.

Example 2

Email sign-off: Regards

Unseen reader reaction can be an annoyed face, interpreting this as a passive–aggressive sign-off: 'Why didn't they write: *Kind regards*?'

Many comment they find this one borderline rude, and the writer can be totally unaware of this. In so many cases it's the last thing they intended.

Example 3

Email sign-off: Kind regards

Unseen reader reaction can be: 'That's old-fashioned, why didn't they write: *All the best?* That's how we show friendliness.'

That said, most incomers to the workplace do seem to agree that some formality is required. It's hard to see a sign-off 'Hugs' (which does happen) as professional, though it's clearly friendly.

Example 4

Email sign-off: Thx *or* Rgds

Unseen reader reaction really can be: 'How rude. Don't I deserve the courtesy of that person taking the time to write the word in full?'

Ditch robotic replies

A major theme of this book is that writing is the new talking. More than ever, this means understanding how to write as a person to a person, and certainly not in a robotic manner. The following email exchange shows what I mean:

Customer: I want to complain about how long my call took to get answered by so-called 'Customer Service' yesterday.

Company reply: No worries. We did experience an unusually high volume of calls yesterday. Hopefully things will be better today.

Unseen reader reaction: 'No worries?' What a ridiculous, robotic response. Can't they sense my frustration? And how exactly is writing 'hopefully things will be better today' relevant to me?

Understand the demographic, write as a person to a person

All these reactions are tasters of real-life office scenarios that can lead to heated discussion topics at home, at work and in online forums. Alongside the pointers I've highlighted, we can add:

1 If we accept we're people communicating with other people, let's show it!

2 Allowing some individual personality in opener and sign-off can be a good idea.

3 For this reason, some businesses have multiple email signatures: some to use internally, some to use externally – which can be particularly important to cover intercultural expectations on formality etc.

4 Follow through in your ensuing writing. Learn to enjoy choosing the right words each time, mindful that even a few words can make a difference for the better!

Judge what works – by once again understanding the demographic and preferred style of your reader where you can. Once the wheels are in motion, you'll find writing so much easier and enjoyable. You'll be more dynamic – and, let's face it, dynamism never stands still.

Activity

Are there any salutations, sign-offs or other expressions commonly seen in emails, that you know:

- routinely irritate you?
- irritate others?

Do jot them down. I have no idea why companies don't encourage employees to do this more often! The answers to effective writing can be right there, in front of us.

You can go further and gain a consensus with colleagues for what to use and what to ditch.

....

....

....

....

....

Email scenarios to watch out for

Sending too quickly

We all do it: type our messages and send without checking. Spelling and grammar mistakes, abrupt tone, overreacting or simply not answering questions can all make readers judge your emails in a negative light. Be prepared to override predictive text that can also result in nonsensical words being suggested, accepted and sent. Take the time you need to get it right. It's an investment in success.

Draft folder

Really pressured? Know you can't send your email by return? Start to craft a reply in your draft folder until you can complete it, maybe after asking someone for help. That's strength – not weakness.

CC (or cc)

The 'cc' is for copying your email to other recipients so they see the same message as the main addressee. Don't copy in people unnecessarily; it can cause information overload. It can also cause confusion, or create anxiety – people can second guess why they're copied in. So explain the reason. If you use a cc internally within your company, it's not generally a problem when those listed in the cc field see others' email addresses. But where your cc field includes the email addresses of external recipients, you may get into trouble because of privacy and data protection laws. You'll know how spammers can also use these lists – and forwarded email addresses can harbour viruses.

BCC (or bcc)

This stands for 'blind carbon copy' where a copy of the email is sent to a recipient whose address cannot be seen by other recipients. It's useful for confidentiality.

Structure your emails

You help everyone including yourself by designing emails that work. So don't type words just as they occur to you, in no particular order:

- without outlining your objectives (even if it's just for information)
- without letting readers know who needs to do what and when

- without attention to punctuation, grammar and accuracy
- with poor layout

Today's readers don't expect to read solid blocks of text. If they don't like the look of a piece of writing, they may intuitively feel they're not going to like its content. This may even prevent them from bothering to read it.

When it comes to our personal email, and the world of blogging, we can relax to an extent. These are areas where we can let our writing just capture our thoughts as they spill out (though we still have to observe the constraints of the law, including libel etc). Readers are more likely to have the time and the inclination to read our outpourings and storytelling – but this approach is definitely best avoided for business email.

Leave some white space by using paragraphs for new topics; people will thank you for it because, by and large, people like that – not least because we approach reading by scanning.

Make the purpose, the time frame and any call to action clear to enable people to respond. Naturally, if your email has no purpose, then don't write it!

Design how you write emails

Here are some further guidelines.

Corporate communication

Is there a corporate style regarding layout? Do you have a corporate font? Have you considered readability and accessibility, as I highlighted in Chapter 3? Are you using your spellcheck and grammar check – and have you selected the correct variety of English?

Tone

As you're learning throughout, introduce the right tone for your target audience in each email.

Always remember that if you are not prepared to say a particular thing face-to-face, or if you would not be happy for other people to see your email (including people you may not know about), then don't write it!

Context matters for understanding and decision-making

Some companies believe in stopping lengthy email threads, preferring to start fresh emails. It's very likely though that you might need to carry information over, so consider recapping the key points made previously. Context matters. It's important you supply that if it's in danger of being lost. It's an essential point I'll be revisiting in the coming section on instant messaging.

Let's look at some red flags – analyse for yourself

How would you assess the email thread in the following case study which shows some of the challenges I've highlighted?

CASE STUDY   Dealing with a customer's email complaint: Stage 1

Let's look at this example of some email exchanges regarding a faulty washing machine. Although fictitious, it's close to a real-life scenario a consumer experienced. How well do you think the manufacturer communicated at each stage?

To: Customer Service, XYZ

From: Customer ABC

Complaint re Washing Machine model DEF

Hi,

I'm writing to complain that my new washing machine, model DEF, still under warranty from you, is damaging my clothes during the washing cycle. Please get back to me as a matter of urgency to sort this out.

Regards

Customer ABC

From: Customer Service, XYZ

To: Customer ABC

Washing Machine model DEF

Hi,
Thanks for your email. We've looked into your claim, and we can confirm that model DEF does comply with all our safety standards.

We hope you find this information helpful.

Best wishes,

The Customer Service Team

How would you feel about this Stage 1 written exchange if you were the consumer involved? I would be irritated, because:

- Where is the acknowledgement that the consumer is experiencing a problem?
- Isn't Customer Service's function to empathize, at the very least?
- Where is the realization that it might be a manufacturing rather than a safety problem?
- In fact, did anyone really read the consumer's email? Once again, ineffective writing is so often the result of ineffective reading.

And the very important question is: did the problem end there – or did the complaint escalate? You've guessed, it's the latter!

CASE STUDY Dealing with a customer's email
complaint: Stage 2

To: Customer Service, XYZ

From: Customer ABC

Complaint re Washing Machine model DEF

Hi,
In reply to your last email:

1 I am appalled at this poor customer service on your part.

2 I have telephoned your service department myself and am outraged
that I had to do this. You should have done this on my behalf.

3 One of your engineers has now visited. He reports that the drum in
the machine is faulty and that's why our clothes are torn.

4 I demand a replacement machine asap and want to hear from you
when this will be.

5 I also think some compensation is due for the damage to our
clothes, as well as the inconvenience.

Regards,

Customer ABC

From: Customer Service, XYZ

To: Customer ABC

Washing Machine model DEF

Hi,
Thanks for your latest email and for the update on our engineer's report.

We will arrange for a new machine to be installed at your premises when we have availability.

Assuring you of our best service at all times,

Customer Service Team

What do you think of this exchange? There are so many red flags in the business writing involved!

Let me highlight some of the key ones.

At Stage 2, the customer's continued dissatisfaction is clear. We see that:

1 The customer has organized their email and numbered the five issues they address. The expectation is that the company will afford the courtesy of replying to each point. The company ignores this.

2 The 'Customer Service' reply makes no apology for the fact that 'the left hand didn't know what the right hand was doing'; that is, they should have felt accountability and been the ones liaising with their own technical department's engineer, not left it to the customer.

3 There is no indication that a new machine will be installed as a matter of urgency. 'When we have availability' means nothing to the consumer.

4 There's no mention of compensation or in fact any goodwill gesture, despite the actual damage to clothes caused by the faulty washing machine drum.

5 They never even acknowledge that there is a complaint in their email headings.

6 The sign-off is glib and insincere in view of the circumstances. Have they really offered 'best service at all times'? (The points I made about standard endings in Chapter 2 remain relevant here.)

This serves as a very useful exercise on writing effective emails (and of course other business writing too) – and provides a checklist for you to refer to from time to time:

- Have you *really* read what people have written? As I stress throughout, it's so often the case that effective writing can only follow on from effective reading.

- Do you *really* see things from the other people's viewpoint when you write?

- Do you go further and empathize with their situation as necessary?

- Do you answer *each point* they might raise, systematically?

- Do you take responsibility for trying to get a resolution, even if it means liaising with others in your organization, so you secure the best possible outcome?

- Is your writing fit for the specific purpose, sincere and not just 'cut and paste' trite language?

Although this example relates to customer service, the lessons apply to many business email scenarios.

Before you send

- Re-read your email and check it's correct on every level.
- Have you included any attachments you say you have?
- If you've copied somebody in, have you explained why?
- Is the subject heading good?
- Is the email structured, easy to read/accessible?

After sending

Check after the event (a day, two days, a week, etc) that you achieved the outcome you want.

Instant messaging and texting

Instant messaging (IM) and text messaging (SMS) are some of the fastest-growing areas of business communication and are widely used in social media too.

Both are predominantly text-based but IM is more about real-time, quick-fire replies between two or more correspondents (usually internally within a business, though you can invite external members for specific projects). Unlike with email, settings can be adjusted to identify who is on- or offline, or busy, and alert them to contact you at a mutually convenient time if necessary.

It's a really useful medium where:

- things need to be moved quickly along (for example, sales or financial teams needing the latest figures, or people needing to know quickly about a bump in negotiations)
- teams and communities need to be kept in the loop and can dip in and out of the ongoing newsfeed
- you need group chat or a conference
- those in the group have implicitly given members permission to the effect 'if you haven't heard from me on email or phone, contact me in real time on WhatsApp' (or alternative)

It's also noticeable how newcomers to the workplace can be more comfortable with IM over voice chat in these situations – another reason for its increasing effectiveness in business writing.

Performance challenges to watch out for

We've seen the problems in sending emails too quickly, so it's easy to see how the rapid reply feature of messaging builds in more hazards to avoid. Even if you work in a highly traditional organization, you'll see abbreviated language, emoticons and imprecise spellings, grammar and punctuation which, as we've seen, can sometimes lead to confusion and misunderstandings. What we're also seeing is a growing pressure to make instant decisions, although there are times when this is a bad move. Instant replies shouldn't equate with short-term thinking or what we term 'gut reactions'. Do watch out for this.

On a style level, think this through in your workplace. For example, to what extent do you want the increasingly casual style of IM, where it's quite normal to express emotions via emoticons or even via use of punctuation as much as by words, to cross over into emails and other communication too?

It's been my privilege to help companies assess what to do, and how to keep up, over many years. And I'm fascinated to see that sometimes fairly traditional conversational styles can stand the test of time and varying cultures the best.

It's a good point to discuss with colleagues because we're seeing the business email style (see Example 1 in the box) often change to very or slightly casual textspeak (see Examples 2 and 3).

Example 1

John: Hi. Please may we have a meeting tomorrow?

Jane: Yes, certainly. Shall we say 9.30 am? I look forward to catching up with you.

Example 2

John: U cool with mtg tom?

Jane: Heyyyy no worries CU tom. 9.30. Catch up then lol

Example 3

Josh: Hey, are you around tomorrow for a quick meeting?

Emily: Yeah sure – 9:30 ok?

Josh: Perfect!

Emily: Cool – catch up then!

Example 1 shows a fairly traditional style; Example 2 the style that we saw some years ago, which already looks very old-fashioned; and Example 3 shows what we often see today. But even that will date. 'Cool' already isn't a word that Gen Z and other upcoming generations are likely to use.

That's why I feel that the fairly traditional conversational style in Example 1 is likely to keep the best currency across the ever-changing generations in the workplace and across diverse cultures. Everyone needs to understand your writing and not feel alienated by modern-day slang or colloquialisms that (even unintentionally) can have the undesired effect of putting up barriers – 'you're not in my zone' – or conversely that become dated without you realizing! Inclusive language rejects barrier words that exclude, even unintentionally, and clearly work best in today's and tomorrow's workplace.

A really useful exercise would be for you to have intergenerational discussions in the workplace on this topic. Not enough companies do.

Structure in instant messages and texts

Well, that's just it. As we're talking about real-time or almost immediate communicating, there's not always a lot you can do to structure these! There can be some challenges or at least considerations to take into account. Let me help you navigate through some of the most common.

Missing headlines and context

The absence of the headings that you would give emails can make it more difficult to get the full gist of IM trails.

As one example, I imagine you've seen the 'wrong answers' coming in from your respondent – in the sense that they don't align sequentially with your questions? In fact, do you always wait for an answer to come in when you see the legend '(name) is typing' before typing your next question? Many don't! Then, far from messaging providing the solution, it creates the problem. It's just as important to write effectively in texts and IM as in any other form of writing. Try one question at a time and allow adequate time for the reply you need to arrive.

A common challenge you'll see is where there's a flurry of conversation between members of a task force, for example. Some of the questions and answers soon become hidden in the deluge. The software may be there to help people organize their replies, but you'll see it's often bypassed when people 'are in the moment'.

The danger is that over-reliance on speed means that the dots don't get connected – and this form of writing then becomes ineffective. Messages can not only get out of sequence, they can arrive without the context that explains why they are being sent. It's a new form of having to decode communication – and as with more traditional business writing:

- you might be onto a new task
- you might be distracted (easy in a time of information overload)
- it also might be easier not to bother!

Short attention span and/or ineffective reading

These challenges apply to all business writing today and are arguably most apparent in IM exchanges. Let's look at this example.

A customer had decided to proceed with the purchase of a new car. In one instant message he asked the salesperson:

Customer: I'm hoping to proceed with the purchase today but need your answers on:

What do you think the timeline for delivery is?

When will my order be confirmed?

What options do I have for tyres?

What insurance do I need to bring?

When I have the answers to these questions, please can we arrange to speak?

Salesperson: No worries

And that concluded his input. Nothing more happened until the prospective buyer followed up.

How do you think the buyer felt at this stage?

Let me tell you. He felt ignored and he felt irritated. How should he have felt? Valued. And surely the reason for the way he felt was largely the result of any or all of these attributes shown by the salesperson:

- short attention span
- ineffective reading of, and failure to reply to each point raised
- lack of accountability in following through
- customer disservice

Further speed traps, e.g. increased use of emojis and jargon

In Chapter 3 we looked at some of the problems emojis can cause and in Chapter 7 the problems that jargon and acronyms can cause. Unfortunately, these problems can be found in abundance in IM, not least because of the widespread use of all sorts of short-hand, such as the following, for speed.

One real-life scenario featured the use of the acronym LOD where the task force comprised sales, logistics, supply and IT experts. Problems arose because:

- the sales team took LOD to mean Last Order Date
- the logistics and supply teams took it to mean Left On Dock
- the IT team took it to mean Level of Design/Development/Detail

It obviously leads to misunderstandings in terms of outcomes. In this scenario the reason only became apparent a long way into the process, when just one individual asked: 'What does LOD actually mean here?' Only then was the discrepancy unearthed.

It can be amazing how:

- so many don't understand the shorthand used in IM (which may also be emojis)
- so many don't ask
- so many make assumptions that aren't right

Sometimes you have to write the common denominator

For example, there can be quite heated group IM discussions between people when they see the acronyms KPIs (key performance indicators) and OKRs (objectives and key results). Some see the former as too narrow and stifling creativity while others can, with a passion, prefer the expression OKRs.

The terminology you use can indeed stir up feelings – and sometimes you have to write to be inclusive. IM is not the medium to debate such differences (valid though the discussion is) when it's not pertinent to the task in hand. So I suggest (as in the section on email) that writing in more traditional, standard English can work better in IM too. As everyone should be striving to achieve 'goals and results' maybe they're the best words to write in certain circumstances, where they can work as the common denominator. It's a good point for discussion.

Extra challenges – including those for non-native English speakers

On a very practical level, just as you need to think about your readers' proficiency in English in other writing tasks, don't forget this applies equally in the fast-moving messaging arena. Just because you may be able to fire off, let's say, five points – if not simultaneously, at least in quick succession – doesn't mean your correspondent can reply as speedily. Non-native English speakers frequently comment on this. Understandably they can need extra time to frame their responses. Tune in to the impassioned pleas about this on channels such as LinkedIn.

Other possible barriers to consider

Instant messaging and texting can also create the same sorts of barriers as other jargon does. Can you see the problems when abbreviations can perhaps unintentionally embarrass people into having to admit they actively don't like it or find it inappropriate? They can be equally embarrassed by not understanding it – or having to pretend that they do. So tread with care.

Here are some tips to help:

- Consider a business user policy that's separate from your personal use and which can include status/availability settings (within the system application you use), and whether you use texting and messaging for internal and external use.

- As part of this policy, consider whether sensitive or negative information can or should ever be relayed by this method rather than face-to-face or by formal notification.

- Remember that all written messages can provide an audit trail. Be professional: project company values and quality – and maintain reputation (yours and others').

- Work out which expressions have common currency so readers understand any shorthand you use.

- When you do use emojis use those that are right for your reader.

- As with email, don't let speed trap you into inferior writing. Abbreviated spelling may be acceptable, but each message has to be understood.

- Observe etiquette: just because you are free for those seconds, you might be interrupting someone else's meeting etc, even if their status setting indicates they are available. Ask when they can reply if you don't hear by return.

- Etiquette also involves the right tone – and understanding recipients' preferred style. In a group situation a standard neutral style may work best and stand the test of time.

- As with email, let readers know where the message is leading and what response you need.

- It may be better to deal with one message at a time because of the 'on the go' nature of the medium. Use line breaks to avoid run-on sentences that are difficult to decipher.

- Check whether texting or messaging mode is migrating into your other business communication and what guidelines you may need to have in place to uphold quality and values.

Activity

Discuss the best use of texting and instant messaging with colleagues and how this may impact on your other corporate communication.

Collaborate on the code you will use to avoid misunderstandings, even giving offence.

It's also helpful to decide on the salutations/endings you will use (as required). You might be surprised how important this is in workplaces to avoid irritated readers' faces!

Your checklist for action

This is a surprisingly long list to help you, as there's so little training out there! So take your career forward by asking yourself, before you press send:

- Is email or instant messaging the right communication medium?

- Is your English fit for purpose? E-writing may seem casual but it's still corporate communication and your English has to be professional.

- Have you run a spellcheck and grammar check on your emails, using the correct variety of English?

- If you use predictive text, have you checked the words offered are the ones you mean?

- Have you made the email subject heading relevant so people want to/know they must read it?

- In exchanges, have you refreshed your headings (if appropriate) and updated details that have changed?

- Have you supplied context if needed, so your message makes sense in isolation?

- Did you get to the point using accessible language so readers know where you're leading?

- Did you *systematically* read the points in the email or message to which you are replying?

- Hand on heart, did you *systematically* cover those points?

- Have you overreacted? If you aren't prepared to say your message face-to-face or let it be seen by others, don't send it.

- If you see that someone is typing a response, do you wait for it to arrive before firing off another instant message in the conversation?

- Would it be a problem for you or your organization if this email or message is forwarded in its entirety to other people without your knowledge? Don't forget that all written messages can be used in an audit trail.

- Are you sending the attachments you promised?

- If you're copying someone in, have you explained why?

- Have you developed the right rapport with your readers and met their business and cultural expectations?

- Have you set (and are you remembering to update) your IM status?

- Messaging mode is sure to be migrating into your other more formal business communication, so do you have guidelines in place to uphold quality and values?

- Are you keeping up to date on changing language and punctuation in business writing today? If not, do it from now on – and bring colleagues on board.

- Are you regularly checking that whatever shorthand you use is both relevant and understood by all?

- Equally importantly, are you regularly checking that you understand what others have written?

09
Practical conventions and common confusions

Written conventions are used for a positive reason. Confusions aren't!

This chapter is a guideline for you to understand why conventions can be useful and to watch out for common confusions to avoid.

But it's now over to you to identify your own list to refer to, as I can't know your exact business needs. Take ownership now – and be the author of your ongoing success. Join forces with colleagues too!

So let's start with some common conventions which have originated for a reason, namely for ease of reference and for conveying information accurately.

Dates

Just writing for a home market? You'll know what to write. But if you're dealing internationally, it can be a different matter.

Differing conventions

There are a number of correct ways of writing dates in English. The UK English format (which most of Europe uses) is:

DD/MM/YY, where D = day, M = month, Y = year

This contrasts with the US format:

MM/DD/YY

And both are in contrast with the format used in Japan, for example:

YY/MM/DD

Not understanding differing conventions can create immense problems. If you have to book international transport or hotel accommodation, or arrange deliveries, meetings and so on, you'll know how important it is to input the correct dates. And yes, we all know of things that have gone mightily wrong in this respect!

It can simply be a question of house style regarding the format you choose to be your default convention. But you may need to be flexible and understand customers may be using a different convention. Check if there's any uncertainty. Sometimes be prepared to mirror their convention, as long as it's an acceptable version that makes sense. Being in business should be about embracing customers' needs, not about seeing them as 'awkward' if they do something differently.

Examples that are all perfectly acceptable in UK English are:
21 January 2030
21st January, 2030
21 Jan 2030
21st Jan 2030
21/01/30

As I mentioned, US English uses a month/day/year format, as do some other countries. In this case, write:
January 21 2030
01/21/30

This particular date isn't too problematic because we know that there aren't 21 months in a year. But where readers don't understand the differences between the UK and US conventions, they could have problems with a date such as 03/06/30. In the UK this denotes 3 June 2030, but in the United States it denotes 6 March 2030. It really matters, doesn't it?

International date format

This was devised to make the way we write dates internationally understandable. It is based on the following format:

YYYY – MM – DD

In this format, YYYY refers to all the digits (e.g. 2030), MM refers to the month (01 to 12) and DD refers to the day (01 to 31).

When there's any doubt, it's really useful to write your dates in English this way.

Some confusions

Days and weeks

If you write 'next Tuesday', people can get confused as to whether you're referring to the first Tuesday that follows after the day you wrote this – or whether you mean a Tuesday in another week. So, as an example, if you write it on a Monday, is 'next Tuesday' the following day (which I would take it to mean), or the Tuesday of the following week? If you write it on a Friday, it is easier to see that it would have to be the Tuesday of the following week.

'This coming Tuesday' has the same meaning as 'next Tuesday'. So do be careful. I know of instances where misunderstandings about this have led to missed appointments. Ironically, the people who misunderstand the correct use of the expression are the ones who can get angry. Also, imagine the cost if you book foreign travel for the wrong date. The best arrangement is always to write the precise date you mean, for example: 'next Tuesday, 4th November'.

'In a couple of weeks' literally means 'in two weeks', as 'couple' means 'two' in English. It is true that 'a couple of weeks' can be used in a looser sense, meaning in about two weeks, but it's best to check. As another example, the Dutch expression *paar dagen* means a few days, but the Dutch often wrongly translate this into English as 'a couple' or 'two' days. So where orders are concerned, it's always best to clarify what is meant.

'Next Monday week' means 'a week from next Monday'. 'Over a week' in English means 'in more than a week's time'. But non-NE writers often use the expression 'over a week' to mean in a week's time, that is, one week from now. An example would be: 'The delivery will be over a week.' Again be careful if you are dealing with orders, because you can confuse.

'A fortnight' means two weeks. I find that many nationalities are unaware of this word, so it can be better to avoid it.

Time off

In UK English, people usually refer to their 'holidays', where US English uses 'vacation'. Time off work for holidays is referred to as 'leave'; time off through illness is 'sick leave'.

Public and bank holidays

A public holiday is an official holiday for the majority of a state or country. In the UK, the term 'bank holiday' is used when the public holiday falls on a weekday when banks are closed by law. When you write about public holidays or bank holidays globally, be aware that they can vary from country to country, usually being cultural in origin.

Time

Things can go seriously wrong when different nationalities fail to understand that they may have differing conventions for writing times. People fail to turn up to meetings at the right time, they miss flights and deadlines: in short, if a matter is time bound it can go wrong. And what in business is not linked to time? Here are some guidelines to help.

UK English

All these written versions are correct in English:

The meeting starts at 09.00.

The meeting starts at 9am [or 9 am or 9 a.m.].

The meeting starts at nine o'clock in the morning.

The meeting starts at nine in the morning.

English usage includes both the 12-hour clock (morning and afternoon) and the 24-hour clock (especially for timetables), so:

09.00 means nine o'clock in the morning

21.00 means nine o'clock in the evening

Strangely enough, 24.00 is also 0.00 hours!

If we write in English, 'The meeting starts at half past eight', this could mean 'The meeting starts at 08.30' or 'The meeting starts at 20.30'.

Often, we'll know from context which is correct. For example, if meetings are held during normal office hours, then half past eight in the morning is the more likely time. But say we work in a staggered-hours environment, then it could be a morning or an evening meeting. You need to clarify.

Differing conventions in different countries

Mishaps or missed meetings and other appointments all arise when we fail to realize that the way different countries express time isn't standard. For example, the United States does not generally use the 24-hour clock (except specifically by some professions: for example, the military, the police, the medical profession). Some countries (e.g. Germany) use a format to express half an hour before an hour. This is alien to native English writing – where half past six, for example, should be expressed as 'half seven' to the German way of thinking.

Don't underestimate how problematic failing to appreciate this source of misunderstanding can be. Do ensure that everyone understands how to write and read times in English, for the sake of efficiency.

Numbers

If you are writing numbers in English, also be aware that different nationalities may interpret the numbers differently. Look how your order books – and your bottom line – could be affected. For example, the words 'billion' and 'trillion' can have completely different meanings in the UK, Germany, France and the United States. But a zillion means a large indeterminate number, so that expression at least is standard!

A fairly old imperial expression you will still find on occasion is dozen. It means 12.

You use a comma when you write a number comprising four or more digits. Counting from right to left, you place the comma after each three digits:

1,000
10,000
100,000
100,000,000

This convention doesn't always apply, as you'll see below.

How the decimal point is written in English

'Decimal point' is the UK English term for the dot placed after the figure that represents units in a decimal fraction: for example, 9.6. This may differ from the way you express the decimal point in your language. You may be used to using a comma – for example 9,6 – or you may express 100,000,000 as 100.000.000. It's not overly confusing but it's best to be aware of this difference when you write in English.

Decimal points when writing monetary units in English

Some nationalities express their decimal currencies using commas where there is a decimal fraction: €1,80. If you are writing a tariff in English, you express this amount as: €1.80

Other punctuation differences are apparent in the following written representation of the same number. The UK English version is the first of these:

890,123.50

890.123,50

Measurements

Do you have to write measurements in English? If you're writing globally, be aware that different countries use different systems. Broadly speaking, these are called metric and imperial.

The United States largely uses imperial and the UK and other countries may use a combination. You will need to research if you're involved in orders that use either system. To give you an idea, some differences are as follows:

- Metric system:
  - length: centimetre, metre, kilometre (US spelling: meter etc)
  - weight: gram, kilogram, tonne
  - capacity: millilitre (ml), litre (US spelling: liter etc)
  - temperature: centigrade or Celsius
- Imperial system:
  - length: inch, foot, yard, mile
  - weight: ounce, pound, ton (mainly US) and tonne (mainly UK)
  - capacity: fluid ounce, pint, gallon
  - temperature: Fahrenheit

Even within the imperial system, you'll find that a US ton is not the same as a UK ton, and a US gallon is different to a UK gallon.

Temperatures are also written using different systems:

- Celsius or centigrade: freezing point of pure water 0° (degrees); boiling point 100°
- Fahrenheit: freezing point of pure water 32°; boiling point 212°

Words that can confuse both native English and non-native English writers

Some words repeatedly cause businesses confusion. We looked at some of these in Chapter 7. Sometimes though it's because different people within the same company set their computer spellcheck to different varieties of English. Often homonyms confuse. These are words that have the same sound but can have different meanings and spellings.

As an example the word 'mean' would indicate 'average' in a financial report but indicate 'unpleasant' if referring to a person. An example of a homonym with different spellings is 'compliment' and 'complement'.

Words or spellings that commonly confuse

Here are some common examples. Tune in to those you've seen and know what to add.

Receive/recieve

The correct version is 'receive'. A useful rule in English spelling is that after the letter 'c' the letter 'e' goes before 'i'.

Stationary/stationery

'Stationary' means standing still. For example, 'The careless driver crashed into a stationary car.'

'Stationery' means writing and printing materials. For example, 'I've ordered new business stationery for my office.'

Licence/license, practice/practise

In UK English, the nouns relating to these words end in 'ce'. The verbs end in 'se'. For example:

'Which doctor's practice do you go to?' (Practice = noun: the doctor's place of work)

'You should practise what you preach.' (Practise = verb)

US English is different. 'Practice' (note the *c*) and 'license' (note the *s*) are always the spellings, no matter whether they are nouns or verbs. For example:

'He has a valid license (noun), so he is licensed (verb) to drive here.'

'The best practice (noun) is to practice (verb) what you preach.'

Compliment/complement

'Compliment' is a noun or verb meaning praising or admiring. 'Complement' is a noun or verb meaning a thing that completes something else. For example:

'We are always delighted to receive a compliment from a customer.'

'When dining, the right ambience complements the meal.'

Loose/lose

'Loose' is an adjective that means not tightly packed or fixed. For example:

'There is a loose connection in the wiring system.'

'Lose' is a verb that means cease to have, be unable to find. For example:

'If we lose their parcel we will also lose their custom.'

There/their

'There' is an adverb meaning in that place. 'Their' is an adjective meaning belonging to them. For example:

'The file you need is over there. It will be their turn next.'

Where/were/we're

'Where' is an adverb, meaning in (or to) which place, direction or respect. 'Were' is a verb, the past tense of 'to be'. 'We're' is a contraction of 'we are'. For example:

'Where are we going on holiday?'

'You were at home last night and now you are at work.'

'We're attending a training course today.'

Your/you're

'Your' means belonging to you. 'You're' is the contraction of 'you are'. For example:

'Your bag is in the other room.'

'You're expected in half an hour.'

And although we so often see 'Your welcome' in e-writing responses, it should be 'You're welcome'!

Activity

Make a note of the common confusions that you and your colleagues encounter. Become your own editor at this stage in the book by building the tools you need for communication success throughout your career.

....

....

....

....

....

High word count isn't always linked to productivity!

Many business writers think they must embellish or over-complicate their writing. Even the most effective speaker can seem to feel that to write simply and clearly is a sign of weakness.

It's really not true. Implying 'busyness' in high word count (or multiple mouse movements for tracking purposes) doesn't necessarily indicate productivity. Nobody should be duped into thinking that. Fewer words, if they're the right words, can produce better results.

Also, some people can't break away from thinking that high word count and complex vocabulary signify 'we're cleverer than you'. Historically, intellectual, academic writing, for example, uses nominalization, in which nouns are used in place of verbs. This may be useful in writing about concepts. But in business it can seem pompous and outdated. We saw in Chapter 5 how verbs can create vibrant content – but nominalizations do the complete opposite. These examples show the nominalization first, followed by the clearer verb form:

give clarification on this = clarify this

in recognition of the fact = recognizing that

during the installation process = when installing

we are involved with negotiations = we are negotiating

The verb form gives more energy: we know that something is happening in each case and that people are involved. With nominalization, users appear to hide behind language. That's rarely a great idea in business.

Your checklist for action

- When writing dates, times and measurements, one size doesn't fit all.

- Understand the conventions your readers use.

- If you don't do this, you may miss appointments, delivery deadlines, etc.

- Your order books may be adversely affected if you get dates, times and numbers wrong – your profits too.

- Write as precisely as possible to avoid misunderstandings: for example, 2nd January 2030.

- Define the terms you will be using and check that your readers use the same ones.

- Make sure you write plain English, using words precisely – and approach high word count with caution.

- Look out for the common confusions described in this chapter.

- Very importantly, become your own editor and, on a regular basis, draw up lists of common confusions you and your colleagues encounter so you avoid them in the future.

10

Look to the future

You know when your writing's truly effective, whether it's electronically or on paper. You've drawn the strands together to get the results you need, which includes how your readers feel.

How does writing make readers feel?

Take a look at the world around you and you'll soon pick up on the importance of 'the reader experience'. Even in business writing, we need to check that our readers are feeling the way we want them to feel. I just wonder if you've ever thought about using a multi-sensory approach in your writing. Let me explain how you might.

Naturally, we all use our five senses in differing proportions. We see it in writing too. It's fascinating to tune in to people's individual preference as to whether they write, just as an example:

'I hear what you're saying' (auditory)

'That feels right' (tactile)

'I see what you're getting at' (visual)

On both digital channels and on paper (more about paper shortly), we know how the look and the easiness of accessing information are paramount. Visuals can aid a lot. But as I suggest throughout, it's the written word that will continue to promote our messages – and you've been developing your expertise on how to focus on your reader throughout this book.

This next case study shows how the words we choose can evoke a total experience.

CASE STUDY   Loaf Homeware

Loaf is a British high-street homeware retailer. Over the years it has chosen to communicate in a brand-identifiable, innovative, senses-based and engaging fashion. Check out their website at Loaf.com and you'll get a feel for what I say.

In terms of writing, I'd like you to focus on their use of imaginative descriptive words, such as:

Happy new hues

Crackles of colour and oodles of squish to give your home some oomph

Then note the dynamic verbs that take on equal footing with the products on sale:

Dive into our new collection

Nab some free examples – get stuck in

Smelly wax drops – Take a sniff

Mattresses – Snuggle up

In turn, we find creative word play:

Like the way we Loaf?

This is word play on one meaning of 'loaf'. They use it in the sense: 'stop working and do nothing; chill.' It chimes with the current trend to assess work/life balance. This word play is reinforced throughout:

Stroll by our Shacks – more slow rooms than showrooms

Surrender to life in the slow lane

Listen to the sound of the words too. In short, the Loaf approach is based on enticement. 'Getting comfy isn't just about the seating' – it's also about experiences, such as being a place to relax while reading the paper. The experience of a comfy sofa is 'best served with a mug of tea and a whopping piece of cake.'

While we're not all retailers, in business we do have to sell our messages and, in an age of information overload, 'grab eyeballs', as a business editor of a major international paper once put it to me.

Do you remember I highlighted this in a business context in Chapter 3, in 'the cup of tea' exercise? I asked you to bring out your inner marketer, whatever the writing task. Workplace communication is 'not an island unto itself' – it's got to align with the modern world.

I've really enjoyed helping companies look with fresh eyes at their technical writing, for example. We've revised expressions such as 'It is essential that hard hats must be worn on these premises' to 'Stay safe! Always wear your hard hat on site.' The writing has become conversational and personal.

Stay attuned to this, and stay fresh, whatever you need to write.

Paper is likely to stay around

Although digital writing predominates, paper refuses to fade away, thanks to consumer support. We see books, leaflets, brochures, letters, certain reports, etc continue to play an important role in the business world. In this arena we're seeing fairly traditional, emoji-free writing back in force.

There's consistent feedback that:

- readers have greater recall of print over online messaging
- they revisit it more often
- when it comes to printed mailshots (validly sent to the target audience) readers can feel more valued by any offer you make – they can trust the information more and when delivered to a household, printed material generally can be noticeably more read across generations

The tips I have given you so far in the book will help here, as the writing system I teach works across all writing tasks. That said, I think it would help you to remember four particularly relevant points when it comes to writing for print:

1 Any mistakes you make are likely to be more apparent as readers have more time to focus on errors.

2 Any claims you make can be analysed with greater scrutiny when people have time to reflect on and revisit what you say.

3 If it's a stand-alone piece of writing, with no opportunity for an online, phone or face-to-face chat to clarify things, you can especially see why your words need to say what you mean them to say, in a way that's not open to misunderstanding.

4 For this reason we see a lot of printed material now with QR codes – to provide a very useful link to further information online.

Letters

Business letters today are mostly sent electronically, though we do still find occasions where people like or expect to receive a paper letter. This might be for a legal or financial matter, for orders, for apologies, or an invitation of value and so on.

On the web you will find many suggested layouts to choose from, if your company doesn't already have its own. In order to cover your objectives, you need to identify the purpose of your letter and its possible impact on your reader:

• Is it to inform? If so, why?

• Is it to instigate action? If so, what? Who by? How? When by?

• How do you want the reader to feel when reading your letter? Can your tone assist this?

Do you use a subject heading? Do you use a reference or code? An informative subject heading engages your reader's attention from the start. It also helps you identify the point of your letter. Customize it if you can. Even the use of the word 'your', as in 'Re: your contract XYZ', is more reader-friendly than 'Re: contract XYZ'. (Incidentally, you don't need to use 'Re:' at all; it's a question of house style.)

Third, identify how well your letters work. Ask yourself questions such as these each time:

- Did I achieve the right result from this letter?

- Or was there a problem? Why was that? Was it because of the English I used? What should I have written?

- Did I get no result when I had expected one? Why was that? Should I use English differently next time I write?

When flexibility is key, be prepared to adapt letter-writing

As circumstances change, we need to adapt each writing task. So when it comes to writing letters be prepared to adapt as business expectations evolve. I'll shortly be showing you some creative sub-headings used effectively to illustrate what I mean.

First, be aware that although companies increasingly deal with customer complaints via social media rather than by letter, this still impacts on letter-writing style. It's confusing to have overly different writing styles within organizations. Look at this tweet, sent by a train company to a customer (I've anonymized the details) who had tweeted to complain about a delayed train:

TranscountryRail (@TranscountryRail)
@mariexyz I can see you were 11 mins delayed into London Bridge, I do apologize for this Marie. Jon

We see the apology the complainant expects. But the language is still quite formal if we look at it alongside the language used by a fast-food chain in reply to a complaint by a customer on Twitter (details anonymized) accompanied by a photo of a newly opened bag of crisps (a UK English word – 'chips' in US and other varieties of English):

> Todxyz (@todxyz_)
>
> Are you joking @fastfoodtogo? I was expecting a little more than that when I opened my bag of potato crisps #disappointing
>
> FastFoodToGo (@fastfoodtogo)
>
> @todxyz_ That does look a little stingy! Sorry, did you show our Team Members?

'Stingy' is a colloquial word for 'mean' and denotes 'under-filled' in this context. The informality of social media means readers now expect conversational interaction – where companies aren't afraid to express empathy or say sorry where things go wrong.

If the vocabulary and tone in corporate letters is completely different from a company's social media voice, can you see how this can bewilder readers? It undermines brand consistency – and even credibility. You might 'like' and trust the company's social media voice and 'dislike', even mistrust, a 'formal' letter's distant tone.

Do any of these points strike a particular chord with you or your colleagues? They could make a springboard for wider discussion.

A letter that involves the reader with the company's narrative

You've seen the importance of storytelling in writing for social media and marketing in Chapter 5. We're seeing how an integrated approach to writing tasks can work wonders and as I mentioned earlier, creativity is needed in letter-writing. The fixed templates of yesteryear rarely work.

Even as a start-up you can design simple letters that impress, as the following example letter shows.

Dear Mrs Talbot

How can I help?

We value our customers and we make it our duty to understand their needs and requirements so that we can help them to make their businesses work even better.

Can we do that for you?

Investing a small amount of your valuable time in a brief appointment is all that I ask of you to enable me to understand your business needs, and offer you helpful suggestions as to how you could reduce costs, at the same time as taking your business forward.

Yours sincerely

[Signature and company name]

The simplicity of the message and the development of a two-way relationship (between me and them) made an impact. This agency achieved this by using creative subheadings and by writing 'I', 'we' and 'you' – and yes, it worked: I bought from them.

Even previously 'dry' letters sent, for example, by banks when customers opened accounts can now be lifted by phrases such as:

'A warm welcome to your account'

'We'd like to help you make the most of your account'

'Your security is foremost to us'

This two-way dynamic is becoming more expected in letters that were previously jargon-riddled and convoluted in certain professions. Back in 2018, the Academy of Medical Royal Colleges picked up on the fact that in the UK several million outpatient letters were being sent each month. They were the most-written letters sent in the National Health Service. In their guidance 'Please, write to me' (AMRC, 2018), the Academy went so far as to say doctors have to learn a new skill: writing letters directly to patients in plain English that's well-structured, informative, useful and supportive. It's interesting to note that they also added that it should be *engaging*.

Patients soon fed back comments such as:

'Appreciate the letter addressed to me the patient.'

Or they praised the fact that an understandable, written record to hand really helped, because:

'When you come home from outpatients, you have forgotten what the doctor has told you.'

This was quite a breakthrough; maybe you can think of other professions that would do well to take note.

CVs/résumés and cover letters

Now that you also have a firmer idea of your personal brand, do have a regularly updated CV (also called résumé) as a written overview of your job experience and qualifications. It helps you identify milestones you've achieved, the skills you're developing and the personal attributes you've enhanced. It helps you express what makes you special over and above the next person.

Most CVs are emailed to prospective employers, so once again it's your writing that's judged initially. With stiff competition for jobs, employers can hit hard, often ditching CVs with mistakes or that fail to answer the brief or impress.

Employers see a CV as an applicant's 'sales document'. The most articulate speaker in the world might not get to interview stage, simply because their written words are the weak link. So choose words that describe the skills you can bring to the company. Why are you the perfect fit? Research the company and tailor your writing if you want to get the job.

Professional social networking site LinkedIn (among others) provides great advice and even CV templates to customize for 'brand you'. They show the current way of doing things, as approaches change. Year on year, they list what they term CV 'buzzwords' that have become clichés through over-use, such as: creative, results-oriented, motivated, responsible and so on. None of them are 'bad' words but if everyone uses them, you won't make your mark.

Employers will check your online presence/posts so show them a professional personal brand that will boost your employability. Don't post inappropriate information or discriminatory comments. Reputation matters as much for you as for any company that takes you on.

Include only facts that are true and accurately describe your personal attributes. You must be able to deliver what you say you can.

Cover letter with CV

Some employers like a good covering letter (or email) with your CV. It could improve your chances of getting to interview stage.
Do:

- Show you've done some research on the company. Refer to something relevant on its website, such as its values and goals, expressing how yours align.

- Answer 'Why should you get the job?' by highlighting the special skills you can bring – quantifying results where possible.

- Think of your potential employer (and their likely customers and suppliers), as much as yourself when you write. You've got to persuade and build bridges to get that job!

- Let 'brand you' shine out, to set you apart positively from the rest.

- Show what you expect from a prospective employer as much as what they can expect from you.

- State your availability.

- Run a final spellcheck and grammar check; after all, if English is required in the job, make sure yours is perfect in your application! Ask someone's advice if necessary.

Your checklist for action

- Realize that the one person that can (and should) make the time to invest in your communication success is YOU (yes, I've shouted it on purpose!). Do it.

- Understand that printed material may be scrutinized more and recall may be higher: this also means that mistakes and flawed logic may be spotted more easily.

- Know what you want your written piece to achieve.

- Check that the look and feel of your writing aligns with values shown in other corporate communication. Cohesive writing has authenticity.

- In letters, write your recipient's personal details correctly; use the correct salutation and sign-off; build in rapport and politeness and consider creative subheadings to engage.

- Always remember that it's a person or people you are writing to – and use plain English.

- Represent yourself, your personal brand and your company well.

- Don't make assumptions; write to your brief and for readers' needs. Answer any questions systematically.

- Don't over-complicate your writing, don't use clichés or make false claims.

- Design a CV/résumé that's a 'sales document' for 'brand you' showing writing skills that give you the competitive edge in the information age.

Reference

AMRC (2018) Please, write to me: Guidance, Academy of Medical Royal Colleges, www.aomrc.org.uk/wp-content/uploads/2018/09/Please_ write_to_me_Guidance_010918.pdf (archived at https://perma. cc/563X-GGXH)

CONCLUSION
What will you do differently – and better?

You've got the knowledge now – so what are you waiting for? Grab the opportunity to excel in your business English writing performance – from entry level through to CEO!

You'll remember that I mentioned in Chapter 1 how this book is about helping you navigate your way in the unstoppable digital workplace where writing is the new talking. I listed what effective writing achieves, such as:

- communicating strategy and implementing operations
- developing customer relations and trust
- team collaboration
- diversity and inclusion
- and very importantly, constantly developing 'brand you'

wherever you work, and whatever stage you're at in your career.

Good writing skills will stay in demand, across sectors

To recap a central message: in today's low-attention-span world, you need to get to the point and make sure your writing is understood in the smallest window of opportunity possible. But you still need to:

- make impact and get read
- sell a message, service or product

- influence
- get the desired result
- be seen to be professional

So don't waste your or others' time with waffle, mistakes or messages that have no context.

Own your communication success today and tomorrow!

As mentioned in the Introduction, we're in a world where people barely have time for themselves. If no one else has got time to work on your communication, you'd better seize the opportunity to do it yourself. Now you've got the knowledge to become your own editor!

It's great that artificial intelligence (AI) is providing ever more sophisticated software to help with suggestions on clarity, punctuation, grammar and so on. But it's far from the stage of being able to assess the overall logic and effectiveness of your writing or understand team dynamics etc – and it certainly can't develop 'brand you'. AI can make suggestions, but it will never be accountable. People are. You are.

What has surprised you?

Maybe it's the various levels involved in truly effective business writing. The digital world is so accessible that we can mistakenly think communication is easy. On one level it certainly is, but when it comes to performance and reader relationships it can provide a myriad of hurdles to consider.

Misunderstandings and ineffective communication aren't just common features of intercultural communication challenges when writing globally. They apply almost in equal measure to native English speakers working in traditional or dispersed/hybrid workplaces, even in their home market.

And this can apply from entry level, right through to CEO. The need for performance success never stands still.

Your words need to be understood easily, to convey the meanings you intend them to, provide the information that's needed, at the right time, and enable the results you need.

It's a tall order, isn't it? And it definitely needs a systematic, orderly approach.

Look at the world around you – what do you *now* see?

In Chapter 1, I asked you to picture in your mind someone at work in today's office/home office and I imagined you might well see someone typing or texting. The way business today largely communicates. And communication is the cornerstone, indeed lifeblood, of every organization, large or small.

Right now, taking on board what you've come across in the book, I'd like to ask a slightly different question: 'Close your eyes and capture in your mind the varying reader reactions to business writing scenarios you encounter. What images do you see?'

And there we have it. If your input in terms of your writing gets the right outcomes (on *all* the levels I highlight throughout) then yes, you'll have succeeded. And a very useful metric can be to gauge readers' reactions too.

We've also seen that sometimes it's the 'ordinary' accessible language and some measure of consistency in corporate communication that can stand the test of time – and work best to get those desired reactions.

Stay vigilant – enjoy being a 'style detective'!

This will involve keeping your eyes – and mind – open in four principal ways:

1 Keep on the lookout for examples of effective and ineffective business writing that abound in our daily life. They're not just in the workplace but in the messages we receive as consumers or citizens. Be what I term a 'style detective' – and look for clues in the writing you see. The answers to effective writing will be there, in front of you. You know what to look out for now.

2 See for yourself how every piece of writing can help you shine as a professional. A single line can make a difference for the better if you design it well.

3 Continue to visualize your readers' likely reactions to your writing. If you could see their expressions, what might they be like? What's the experience you're offering? Professional? Logical? Concise? Easily understood? Problem-solving? Interesting? Personable? Empathetic? Inclusive? Relevant to them? Supportive? Complete?

If not, why not?

4 And of course, it's not just your own writing you need to pay attention to. Be vigilant about looking at what others are writing, not least in unguarded threads.

Your personal reset – edit your writing, own your success

What will you do differently and better? You have the tools, you have the confidence. Get excited about making improvements!

Jot down some thoughts on where to begin, right here, right now. For instance, just to start you off, answer the questions in the box.

Activity

1 What are the Top Ten Takeaway Tips you want to work on?

2 What words would you add to the power words list in Chapter 3?

3 What 10 words sum up your personal brand?

4 What 10 words sum up a business brand that you would be proud to represent?

5 What points are you planning to discuss with others after reading this book?

....

....

....

....

....

In this way, you will actually be continuing to close the skills gap between where you were when you started the book and where you are now. Then don't stop there! Chart your progress in the future and pat yourself on the back when you make improvements so you get to where you want to be.

Enjoy using the #WordPowerSkills system to help you create a great 'reader experience' – across all sectors, cultures and generations you encounter.

I wish you success every step of the way!

INDEX

NB: page numbers in *italic* indicate figures or tables

abbreviations 125, 144, 150
academic vs business writing 16–17
accessibility 35–36, 52
acronyms 125–26
activities
    bad writing, identifying 12
    business English, defining 102
    confusions, common 164
    descriptions, powerful 70
    emails, expressions in 136
    emojis 25
    grammar 113
    instructions, writing 34
    jargon 126
    LinkedIn headlines, writing 84–85
    misunderstandings, identifying 119
    nuances 124
    personal reset, your 183
    power words 48
    punctuation 105–06, 113
    purpose, your 10
    quality, in writing 62
    social media, writing for 95
    texting/instant messaging 151
    writing tasks, your 15
Adidas 71
algorithms 73, 82
alliteration 89
anglicized words 101
Apple 89
asterisks 107
attention spans, declining 2, 17, 121,
    179
audience, your 6–7
autocorrect 66

bank holidays, referring to 158
'banter' 24
'barrier words' 23
Bartlett, Steven 76–79
blogs 86–87, 138
body language 11–12

boss, being the 52–53
    gravitas 53–54
    inclusivity 52
    positivity 53
boss, impressing your 48–51
    minutes 49
    reports 49–50
brackets, using 110
'brand you' 58, 84
Branson, Richard 88, 104
British vs US English 99, 122
bullet points, using 110
bullying, workplace 24, 130
business-to-business (B2B) social
        platforms 76
buzzwords 125

calls to action, using 90–91, 138
captions, on social media 68, 85,
        86, 89
case studies
    Bartlett, Stephen 76
    complaints, customer 139–40,
        141–42
    connecting 51
    descriptions, powerful 69
    L'Oréal 31
    Loaf Homeware 168
    Nationwide 93–94
    Octopus Energy 36–37
    Paphitis, Theo 79–80
    Pizza Express 74
    Samaritans 72
    simplicity 44
    style, choosing your 26–27
    Van-Tam, Jonathan 39–41
cc/bcc fields 137
Chinglish 100
cliches 84, 123, 175
'clickbait' 81
closed questions 112–13
Coca-Cola 71–72, 89

commonly confused words 161–64
community, building a 79–80
complaints, customer 11
    by email 139–42
    on social media 83, 92, 171–72
conversation vs broadcasting 73,
        77, 78
Covid-19 pandemic 39–41
creativity, on social media 86
cultures, different 116–18
    cultures that say 'no' 117–18
    cultures that say 'yes' 116–17
curtness, avoiding 23
CV, your 42–43, 174–75
    cover letters 175–76

data protection 130
dates, writing 155–58
decimal points 160–61
departments, different strengths
        of 34–35
Diary of a CEO, The 76
'digital storytelling' 81
direct-to-consumer (D2C) social
        platforms 76
Dragons' Den 76–78
Dunkin' Donuts 89
dyslexia 61, 79, 104

effective written communication,
        defining 27–28
Einstein, Albert 7
ellipses 106–07
emails
    accessibility in 35
    cc/bcc fields 137
    checking before send 136, 143
    complaints, customer 139–42
    headline, your 132–33
    hybrid working 34
    personality, showing 135–36
    reach 129
    in recruitment 43
    replies 135
    salutations/sign-offs 133–34
    structure 137–38
    style 129, 130, 138
    threads 139
    tone 131, 138–39
    upcoming generations, use by 42

variant punctuation 104–08
    when to use 131
emojis 24–25, 150
emotions 88–89
English as a foreign language
        (EFL) 99–100
English as an acquired language
        (EAL) 99–100
English as a second language
        (ESL) 99–100
English for speakers of other languages
        (ESOL) 99–100
English Project's History of English
        Punctuation, The 102
expletives 24, 83

Facebook 75, 83–84
    authenticity on 83
    Pizza Express offer 74
    recruitment on 43
    replying 84
font size 36
formality 12–13, 24, 26–27
Friends Reunited 81
full stops 105

Google 73
grammar 1, 22, 108–09
    mistakes 59
    pronouns 108–09
    proofreading 65–66
graphics, on social media 68
gravitas 53–54
group chats 144

Happy Sexy Millionaire 79
harassment 130
hashtags 71–72, 82
headlines, compelling 74
    in emails 132–33
    in instant messaging 146–47
Hoffman, Greg 77
homonyms 60–61, 66, 162
house style, following 17, 19, 48, 53
'human touch', the 17, 18–19
hybrid working 34, 130

idioms 122–23
inclusivity 52
infographics 68, 89

Instagram 75, 85–86, 115
    captions on 85
    recruitment on 43
instant messaging
    abbreviations 148–49, 150
    emojis 150
    headlines 146–47
    hybrid working 34, 130
    jargon 148–49, 150
    in recruitment 45
    replies 147–48
    style 129, 145–46, 151
    threads 146–47
    upcoming generations, use
        by 41–42
    variant punctuation 104–08, 145
    when to use 144
international date format 157

jargon 17, 30, 123, 125, 173
    in instant messaging 148–49, 150
job-seeking 42–43, 174–76

KitKat 89
Klin, Celia 105

letters, writing 170–71
    CV cover letters 175–76
LinkedIn 75, 76, 84–85
    cliches on 84
    job-seeking 175
    recruitment on 43
    selling on 84
lists 88, 110
Loaf Homeware 168
L'Oréal 31

Manglish 100
Marketing Genius Behind Nike,
    The 77
measurements, writing about 161–62
microblogs 87
minutes, writing up 49
mistakes
    avoiding 59
    credibility, effect on 62–65
    grammatical 59
    miscommunications 118–19
    mistranslations 100
    printed communications 170

social posts 82
speed, risks of 59, 82, 147, 148–49
spelling 59
tone 60
word, incorrect 59, 60–61
mobile content 70, 87
money, writing about 160–61
multigenerational workplaces 41–42
    and social media 78
Mulvey, Christopher 102, 103
MySpace 81

National Health Service (NHS) 174
Nationwide 44, 52, 93–94
native English (NE) speakers 100
    complacency, avoiding 127
neurodiversity 25, 61
newsletters 86–87
Nike 89
nominalization 165
non-native English speakers 98,
    99–100
    advantages for 127
    challenges for 120–22
    instant messaging 149–50
    mergers and acquisitions 118
nuances 124
numbers, writing 160–61

objectives, for social media posts 73
Octopus Energy Group 36–37
offensive language 24, 83
Ogilvy, David 7
open questions 112–13
outsourcing, and responsibility 72

Paphitis, Theo 79–80
paragraphs 110
patronizing, being 17
PayPal 89
personality, showing 135–36
Pinterest 75
Pizza Express 73, 74
podcasts 87
positivity 53, 108, 132
power words 38, 46–48, 47
    on social media 69
predictive text 136, 152
printing presses, impact of 102
print, writing for 169–70

proofreading 65–66
'pseudo-anglicisms' 101
public holidays, referring to 158
punctuation 102–08
  standard 103–04
  variant 104–08
    asterisks 107
    ellipses 106–07
    full stops 105
    'textisms' 105
purpose, your 8–10

QR codes 170
questions, writing 111–13
  open vs closed questions 112–13
quotes 89

'reader experience', the 167–69
readers, your 6–7
recruitment 43–45
  candidate experience, the 45
Reddit 75
reports, writing 49–50

salutations 133–34
Samaritans 72
search engine optimization
  (SEO) 73, 75
sensory writing 167
sentence length 110
sharing, encouraging 82, 88–89, 90
sign-offs 133–34
Singlish 100
Small Business Sunday 79–80
SMS messaging 144
  'textisms' 105
Snapchat 43, 75
social content, updating 70, 75
social platform, choosing the right 75
'social signals' 73
spam 81
Specht, Ilon 31
speed, risks of 59, 82, 147, 148–49
spelling 59
  proofreading 65–66
  spellcheck, using 12, 65–66, 99,
    176
'standard' English 98–99
standard letters 19–23
storytelling 172–74
  'digital storytelling' 81

by email 138
on social media 71, 91–94
structure 110
  in emails 137–38
subheadings 110
swearwords 24, 83

target readership, your 6–7
technical writing 36–39
text messaging (SMS) 144
  'textisms' 105
threads, and context 139, 146–47
TikTok 75, 86, 115
  captions on 86
time off, referring to 158
times, writing 158–60
time zone, and social posts 82
tone 60, 92
  consistency of 171–72
  in emails 131, 138–39
'toxic' workplaces 33, 45,
    53, 107
translations, issues with 120–21
trending topics 82
trust, building 6, 91
Twitter 75, 81, 87
  recruitment on 43

UK vs US English 99, 122, 162
'upcoming generations' 41–42, 80,
  146
user-generated content (UGC) 81

Van-Tam, Jonathan 39–41
verbs, using 165
viral, going 8, 45, 68, 81, 92
  on Facebook 83
Virgin 88
visuals, on social media 68
vlogs 87

website, driving traffic to your 91
WeChat 75
WhatsApp 75
Word Power Skills, steps of 29–30
writer's block 88
writing tasks 15

YouTube 75
  on Facebook 84
  recruitment on 43

CPSIA information can be obtained
at www.ICGtesting.com
Printed in the USA
JSHW041441160523
41794JS00010B/89